Shifting Cultural Power

THE NCCAKRON SERIES IN DANCE

The NCCAkron Series in Dance
Christy Bolingbroke, Editor

Hope Mohr, *Shifting Cultural Power: Case Studies and Questions in Performance*

Shifting Cultural Power

Case Studies and Questions in Performance

Hope Mohr
with contributions from
participants in The Bridge Project

Foreword by Michèle Steinwald

The University of Akron Press
Akron, Ohio

ISBN: 978-1-62922-117-5 (paper)
ISBN: 978-1-62922-118-2 (ePDF)
ISBN: 978-1-62922-119-9 (ePub)

A catalog record for this title is available from the Library of Congress.

∞ The paper used in this publication meets the minimum requirements of ANSI/NISO
Z39.48–1992 (Permanence of Paper).

Cover illustration: "Rings (Coordinated Movement)," Micah Kraus
Cover design by Amy Freels

Shifting Cultural Power was designed and typeset in Garamond Premier Pro by Amy Freels
and printed on sixty-pound natural and bound by Bookmasters of Ashland, Ohio.

Produced in conjunction with the University
of Akron Affordable Learning Initiative.
More information is available at
www.uakron.edu/affordablelearning/.

Contents

Note on Engaging with this Book

This book offers a range of formats. The case studies may be read in sequence or on their own and out of order. For those interested in a behind-the-scenes "underview" of the who and how of the past ten years of The Bridge Project, please refer to the Annotated Archive that begins on page 100. For dancers, students, teachers, and choreographers interested in prompts for studio practice, please refer to the workbook section, "Grounding Politics in the Body: Prompts for Studio Practice," beginning on page 89. Readers and movers can engage with these prompts for embodied practice in conjunction with the book's case studies or as a line of movement research independent of the rest of the book.

This book is dedicated to the artists and thinkers who participated in and contributed to The Bridge Project 2010–2020 on stage and behind the scenes and to those who carry this work forward.

Affinity Project, Larry Arrington, Hannah Ayasse, Zulfikar Ali Bhutto, Byb Chanel Bibene, QTBIPOC Performing Artist Hive,¹ Becca Blackwell, Corey Brady, Marc Brew, Jennifer Brody, Trisha Brown, Barbara Bryan, Rebecca Bryant, Sarah Cecilia Bukowski, Judith Butler, Christy Bolingbroke, boychild, Nigel Campbell, Gerald Casel, Sherwood Chen, Sarah Chenoweth, Lucinda Childs, Tristan Ching, Sandra Chinn, Maxe Crandall, Chibueze Crouch, Sofía Córdova, Jaime Cortez, Gregory Dawson, Thomas DeFrantz, Sammay Dizon, Zoe Donnellycolt, Yalini Dream, Aruna D'Souza, Jeanine Durning, Laura Ellis, Alex Escalante, Jesse Escalante, Lisa Evans, Katie Faulkner, Molissa Fenley, Traci Finch, Aura Fischbeck, Dudley Flores, Amy Foote, Simone Forti, Christy Funsch, Marlene Garcia, Daria Garina, Liz Gerring, Tracy Taylor Grubbs, Miguel Gutierrez, Jack Halberstam, Anna Halprin, Rosemary Hannon, Emily Hansel, Deborah Hay, David Herrera, Leslie Heydon, Cherie Hill, Kristin Horrigan, Xandra Ibarra, Monique Jenkinson, Tammy Johnson, Safi Jiroh, Yayoi Kambara, Deborah Karp, Peiling Kao, Debby Kajiyama, Maurya Kerr, David Kishik, Richard Kim, Nicole Klaymoon, Heather Kravas, Jos Lavery, Claudia La Rocco, Cheryl Leonard, Liz Lerman, Diane Madden, Nicole Maimon, Joanna Mandel, Sara Shelton Mann, Amy Miller, Janice Mirikitani, Paloma McGregor, Rashaun Mitchell, Julie Moon, Maurice Moore, Ranu Mukherjee, Parker Murphy, Jose Navarrete, Megan Nicely, Michael Orange, Phoenicia Pettyjohn, Susan Rethorst, Estrellx Supernova, Frances Richard, Silas Riener, Stephanie Skura, Alva Noë, Michael Orange, Onye Ozuzu, Chrysa Parkinson, Jocelyn Reyes, Maryam Rostami, Aisha Shillingford, Michèle Steinwald, Bhumi B. Patel, Jenny Odell, Nicole Peisl, Jarrel Phillips, Karla Quintero, Yvonne Rainer, Danishta Rivero, Janice Ross, Judith Sánchez Ruíz, Aisha Shillingford, Raissa Simpson, Suzette Sagisi, Dazaun Soleyn, Amara Tabor-Smith, Erin Mei-Ling Stuart, Jenny Stulberg, Lauren Simpson, Nadhi Thekkek, Julie Tolentino, Beatrice Thomas, Snowflake Towers, Dušan Týnek, Edgar Villanueva, Sophia Wang, sam wentz, Maureen Whiting, Taja Will, Tyese Wortham, Megan Wright, Netta Yerushalmy, Stacey Yuen.

Note from NCCAkron

Christy Bolingbroke, Executive/Artistic Director at the National Center for Choreography at The University of Akron

It is not what we do, but how and why we do it.

In 2016, I accepted what would be a liberating invitation to helm the second choreographic center of its kind in the country. Established a year earlier, the National Center for Choreography at The University of Akron (NCCAkron) was founded to support the research and development of new work in dance by: strengthening the national dance ecosystem as an anchor development space for dance; exploring the full potential of the creative process in dance and all its forms; and serving as a catalyst for artistic, cultural, and community advancement and enrichment.

Continuing to acknowledge the tremendous privilege this position affords me to focus on process over product, I also saw this as an opportunity to be a type of organization unto itself. Neither an artist, funder, nor presenter, we may be perceived as any of these ecological players depending on the context and audience. Operating from what I often describe as the cracks in the dance ecosystem, we are more nimble than most organizations. I feel we have a higher threshold for uncertainty, experimentation, and embracing failure. We can improvise as we constantly seek to improve.

Also in 2016, I was fortunate to hear Black postmodern choreographer Ishmael Houston-Jones reflect on his curation for *Lost & Found: Dance, New*

York, *HIV/AIDS*, *Then and Now* with Danspace Project's artist-curated Platforms. Houston-Jones spoke of curating from a place of absence. Others may define curation as the selection of artists, but Houston-Jones' comments have stuck with me as a charge to read the landscape and ask, who is missing?

Upon arrival in Akron, I found the region has a deep history with dance because of a longtime relationship with white male choreographer Heinz Poll and the now defunct Ohio Ballet. In the 1980s and 90s, Poll was a visionary commissioner for the times, inviting in modern dance choreographers to make work for his chamber ballet company. From my vantage point, when Heinz Poll and Ohio Ballet passed on in the early 21st century, the aesthetic conversation around dance somewhat faltered in the city. So my curatorial approach has been to respond to what is missing; to expand the definition of dance through who we invite into Akron for residencies and labs.

This remains a consistent practice when collaborating and working with the dance program at The University of Akron too. NCCAkron moved into what would have been Ohio Ballet spaces on The University of Akron's campus. This location means we have access to various university facilities and resources despite not being part of the university system. Because of NCCAkron's proximity to higher education and the professionalized dance field, I acutely feel the need to evolve dance curriculum on a foundational level. Most dance programs across the county were formed by white men and women (mostly women) before the civil rights movement. As such, the damaging technique binary of ballet/modern continues to be perpetuated because of its own roots in systems of white supremacy. So I have worked to use what NCCAkron can bring to augment the dance program offerings for today's students as well as to locate dance in conversations across campus to tap those faculty and expand who might find dance relevant.

Reorganizing Ourselves, an event with choreographer Deborah Hay, philosopher Alva Noë, and curator Michèle Steinwald, is another artistic experience that shapes my curatorial thinking and operations. *Reorganizing Ourselves* was presented in 2015 in San Francisco as part of The Bridge Project, a platform originated, and that year curated by, choreographer Hope Mohr. During the event, Hay proposed that we should ask different questions rather than seek out the same answers. Noë offered that the Socratic method was not intended to be a new conversation style, but rather a way of using questions to disrupt conversational habits. He proposed that perhaps choreography is not just a means to make dances, but rather a way of disrupting dance-making habits. The seventy-plus people in attendance then physically reorganized ourselves from theater-style seating into one large circle, and Steinwald invited everyone to offer a question. Round and round we went for almost an hour. No answers were offered. A large collection of questions amassed. The weight and volume of those questions were guiding instructions and future prompts alone. But I appreciated the great awareness and working knowledge developed just from listening and reflecting on everyone else's questions.

Since then, my curatorial approach has been to ask new questions in addition to responding to what is missing. Continuing with the unique opportunity and privileges afforded me, I strive to test our capacity to flex and be nimble. As NCCAkron works to strengthen the national dance ecosystem and simultaneously serve as a catalyst for advancement, conversations with artists and observations across the country raise questions concerning the creation of work, its audience, and its broader purpose. In particular: how can we invest in and augment other aspects of the field at large?

The cultivation of dance writing is one experimental way to explore this question. In 2017–18, NCCAkron hosted a year-long Low-Residency Dance Writing Lab including writers from across the country: Sima Belmar (Berkeley, CA), Betsy Brandt (St. Louis, MO), Kathryn Dammers (Philadelphia, PA), Benedict Nguyen (Brooklyn, NY), and Lauren Warnecke (Chicago, IL). We identified these dance writers through an open call and application process. They came from many different perspectives both in and outside of academia. Together we wrestled with and ruminated on what dance writing is and what it could be:

- A piece of art in its own right?
- Power?
- A documentation of ephemerality?
- Validation?
- An extension of the artist? Or for the artform?
- About seeing dance "right or wrong"?
- Advocating for the audience or for everyone other than the audience?
- A by-product of the dance itself?

That year, the Low-Res Dance Writers tried on different ways of writing about dance—playing with form, limitations, audience, print versus online output, etc. Besides the series of products and written exercises produced, two process-based outcomes also emerged that year: (1) a social network with alternative streams of distribution based on the relationships among these writers created a whole other platform where they not only engaged with but also invited each other to publish work across their individual communities; and (2) the ongoing responsibility that accompanies the privilege of writing about an artist's work.

The Low-Res Dance Writing Lab also illuminated some other cracks in our ecosystem. We received more applications from dance writers than any other opportunity NCCAkron had offered. While demonstrating proof of concept, this also showed the dearth of spaces to nurture, convene, and support dance writing. One of the Lab's opportunities included convening the group in New York City around the Association of Performing Arts Professionals conference (APAP). Although this is a major event in the field, most of these writers had not attended before. Even though APAP offers the potential to attend ten-plus festivals in a single weekend and witness numerous dance artists firsthand, the prevailing business of dance touring often discourages potential advocates like dance writers from engaging. They could not easily see anywhere they would be welcome, valued, or able to engage if they were not directly tasked to write a review.

NCCAkron cannot just live inside the cracks of our ecosystem. We must also stretch to fill in some of those gaps and build a stronger foundation for all to dance upon. The Low-Res Dance Writing Lab experience revealed the many different roles that dance writing could play. The immediate possibilities of archive and documentation were intensified by the responsibility NCCAkron can embody as an advocate for undertold and lesser-seen stories in the dance field. In addition to creating more opportunities to share or distribute this new working knowledge, I am also personally interested if we can push for a more conversational and welcoming style of writing about dance, akin to creative nonfiction. It was with these beliefs that NCCAkron entered a series partnership with The University of Akron Press and its director, Jon Miller.

Hope Mohr, who had curated and presented the *Reorganizing Ourselves* event that had so affected me a few years before, was one of the first people I approached to join our foray into dance writing. I first witnessed Hope Mohr's choreographic work in 2012, at her invitation to attend The Bridge Project's performances that year. Shortly thereafter, Hope was brought on as a three-year Resident Artist at ODC Theater. We began and continued a collegial friendship—questioning the relationship her choreographic work had to The Bridge Project itself and seeking to evolve the administrative infrastructure supporting both her choreography and the curatorial platform. We knew the ten-year anniversary of The Bridge Project was approaching in 2020. While a benchmark moment, it also made us ask what such an achievement means. What value could noting this moment have for the future of the dance ecosystem?

In this book—edited by Michèle Steinwald, also of *Reorganizing Ourselves*—I appreciate how Mohr both documents ten years of public programs for choreographers and dance students to reference and also reflects on shifts in power in the cultural sector at large. She makes visible the evolution of operating context. The Bridge Project was originally about creating critical discourse and dialogue within the Bay Area dance community and bridging that work with artists elsewhere (primarily in New York City). In its more recent state, the curatorial platform has been steadily building another bridge (or an entire highway system) between the role of artist and activist.

I invite you to read this book and ask new questions. How is your operating context—your community—shifting? Who, and what, is missing? Who has the power? How can we challenge what we think we know? What experiments to shift within your own power might you make? NCCAkron and I are here to support all aspects of the creative process in an effort to foster the manifestation of new choreographic work and a stronger dance field as we continue to evolve towards more liberated thinking, making, and dancing.

Foreword
Curating Oneself Out of the Room
Michèle Steinwald

I have long craved practical, hands-on language describing curatorial processes in the performing arts, particularly for dance programming. *Shifting Cultural Power* is a dream come true. In this book, Hope Mohr takes an honest, disarming approach to mapping out the stories within The Bridge Project, resulting in a refreshingly relatable publication that is part handbook, part archive, a pinch of memoir, and complementary somatic explorations.

In January 2015, Christy Bolingbroke, then the Deputy Director for Advancement at ODC Theater in San Francisco, introduced Mohr and me. We were all in New York City for the Association of Performing Arts Presenters (now the Association of Performing Arts Professionals, aka APAP) conference. Bolingbroke and I had been in conversation around presenting *Reorganizing Ourselves*, a three-hour, salon-style think tank I codesigned and facilitated, incorporating two performative lectures, one by Judson Dance Theater choreographer Deborah Hay and the other by Bay Area philosophy professor Alva Noë. She knew that including out-of-towners (Hay and me) in her season programming at ODC would be a hard sell, even with a renowned artist such as Hay.

Bolingbroke wisely steered Mohr and me toward one another, knowing that my collaboration closely aligned with Hope Mohr Dance's curatorial platform, The Bridge Project. The early years of The Bridge Project centered on influential Judson-era choreographers Yvonne Rainer, Lucinda Childs, and Simone Forti, alongside Bay Area dance makers; adding Hay's performative lecture was in keeping with that model. Our first meeting led Mohr to incorporate *Reorganizing Ourselves* into The Bridge Project's 2015 program, *Rewriting Dance*. Mohr and I have been colleagues and supporters of one another's work, albeit from a distance, ever since.

Moved by what I was seeing and reading in The Bridge Project's annual programming announcement emails, I was particularly struck by its 2017 *Radical Movements: Gender and Politics in Performance*, which came out just as the #MeToo movement was going viral. Most of us had been expecting America's first female president to be in office and were still reeling from the election. The collision of gender and politics gave us an urgent reason to curate. Between the artists' names and photos listed, gender representation in that issue was broadly displayed and defiantly redefined for a general public. The platform's curatorial backbone was firmly asserted.

At the time, I deeply wished I could fly to San Francisco, attend *Radical Movements*, and experience the performances and dialogues firsthand. I would have loved to witness how audiences participated from their seats, to feel the room, the resonance between the artists and audience members in real time. Flash forward: this book offers the next best thing, including somatic prompts for relating kinesthetically to the concepts behind The Bridge Project's curatorial programming.

While *Radical Movements* marched on, the male gaze continued to invade society as well as performing arts offerings in my local community. Time was pressing for a curatorial platform to speak directly to feminism and matters concerning consent. Mohr's thoughtfulness was evident in 2017's artistic planning. *Shifting Cultural Power* catalogues the circumstances around *Radical Movements* within The Bridge Project's entire programmatic history.

Mohr interviewed me for her blog, *the body is the brain*, in response to my 2018 APAP conference session with choreographer Dr. Ananya Chatterjea entitled "Decolonizing Curatorial Practice 101." During the conversation, I shared some core resources I had learned to lean on to start undoing white supremacist thinking in my curatorial work. I talked about the need to reprogram myself and embody accountability through my practices. We also spoke of tangible ways, as a former dancer and choreographer myself, I could unravel binary rationales that limit my perception of aesthetics and artistic development.

As it happened, at the time of that interview I was preparing for another APAP session, "Artists Building a Code of Ethics in the Era of #MeToo," with theater director Emily Marks in 2019. While I had long admired voices in movements for social change, I had primarily stayed in the wings, as a producer, since retiring as a performer. I had felt more confident in my role behind the scenes. Mohr and I talked honestly and easily over the phone that day, but I still felt vulnerable committing my responses for public scrutiny. Sharing my internal processes turned out to be worth the risk. The resulting blog post, "Building Accountability in the Dance Field," spoke to other justice-minded artists when I posted it on Facebook and is still one of my proudest career markers to date. As she did in her shorter-form written work, Mohr boldly aligns the professional and the personal within the historical through line of her book, including many of the ideas discussed in our interview.

In January 2020, Mohr and Bolingbroke, now director at the National Center for Choreography at The University of Akron, invited me to be this book's dramaturge and support its development as an outside eye by offering conceptual feedback.[2] Because I, personally, have been fed by how Mohr's curiosity and humanity are made evident in her curatorial platforms, the choice to be involved as an editor for the book was an easy one. It's clear the accumulation of The Bridge Project's events and community interactions have been guideposts for Mohr's curatorial journey.

While I would characterize my own curatorial approaches as interventions—unlike Mohr's sustained interactions—I, too, am grappling with how to employ a complicated set of privileges as a white, educated, cis-gendered, queer woman over the course of a career. With social justice and racial equity as the undergirding values within my current curatorial approaches, I know that someday soon, if I am true to my morals, I will be curating myself out of the room. As an activist curator, I have made my motives visible and relied on grassroots political organizing. I aspire to reparations, not just diversity and inclusion. Even as the structures I create around presenting dance become hospitable, resonant, and accessible to more than just white artists, I, as the curator, increasingly become an obstacle for BIPOC leadership. The rationale around being a "woke" white curator holding space for artists of color is ultimately self-aggrandizing. Once my ability to infiltrate white systems of power is no longer necessary, the best I can hope for is to discreetly leave. Like a painter finishing the floor of a room with only one door, I need to head for the exit in order to avoid painting myself into a corner.

ABOUT MICHÈLE STEINWALD

Marked by four major influences (seeing Rosas at age fourteen, producing a post-punk show at age fifteen, studying with Deborah Hay at age twenty-one, and watching for decades the TV series Law & Order), Michèle Steinwald is a Canadian, feminist, DIY, artist-centered, pseudo-forensic, embodied, community-driven, cultural organizer working in the US.

Prologue
What Does It Mean to Have a Radical Body?

Before diving into case studies, I want to share a program note from The Bridge Project in 2017, *Radical Movements: Gender and Politics in Performance*. I wrote this program note in response to the same prompt I offered all of the participating artists in the festival: What does it mean to have a radical body? I offer this program note here to ground the work of shifting cultural power in the body. I also offer this note in the spirit of anchoring curatorial practice in questions. In this way, curating becomes an invitation into critical thinking. The following note was included in the program at all public events in the 2017 *Radical Movements* festival: performances, audience salons, and discussions.

WHAT DOES IT MEAN TO HAVE A RADICAL BODY?

Program Note for Radical Movements:
Gender and Politics in Performance Fall 2017

"Definition is both the problem and the apparent
lifeboat in the storm." —Ariel Goldberg[3]
the dancing body the horizontal body
Can part of the body be radical if other parts are not?
Can you transmit your radical body to someone else?
the body in transition the joyful body
"What does not belong in this world is the only
thing worth making." —Paul Chan[4]
The radical body is unfinished.
Churning. Spinning. Dreaming.
From the Latin *radicalis* "of or having roots." US youth slang use
is from 1983, from 1970s surfer slang meaning "at the limits of control."
Reversing. Reorienting.
Just because something is new doesn't mean it's radical.
Just because you have radical aesthetics doesn't mean you have
radical politics. And vice versa. the outraged bodies in public assembly
Radical movement can come from the left or the right.
If there is no unified we, what does that mean for movement building?
the exhausted body the homeless body
Sometimes I need you to imagine what I'm capable of being.
Improvising. Shaking shit up.
Radical is context-dependent.

What is radical to me might be ordinary to you.

the body that acts before the mind is ready the body that

insists on pleasure

Is my body radical if I think it is?

Does radical need an audience to be radical?

the ambiguous body

"What are the categories through which one sees?" —Judith Butler[5]

Abstraction can feel radical if you're expecting narrative.

the body that refuses to go numb the body that is not a market niche

Radical bodies leave potential in their wake.

the aging body

Radical movement forces us to ask: what next?

the body that is not afraid[6]

Chapter 1

Curating as Community Organizing
What it Means and Why it Matters

*To learn which questions are unanswerable, and not to answer them: this
skill is most needful in times of stress and darkness.*
—Ursula Le Guin[7]

This is a book for movement artists and cultural workers who are interested
in shifting cultural power. Because white people have monopolized cultural
power for so long, this book is especially for white people. African American
visual artist Rashid Johnson notes how whiteness, like any racial category, is
not monolithic:

> I don't believe there is a white gaze that we can speak about without delving
> into the complexity of whiteness. What whiteness are we talking about? Is
> it the white liberal? The white New Yorker? Is it European whiteness? Is there
> a privilege that is also qualified by a real financial agency as opposed to
> poverty? This produces different kinds of perspectives.[8]

For cultural shift to happen, white people need to talk to other white people
about giving up power. For too long, people of color have been called upon to do
this educational and emotional work. Feminist writer Judit Moschkovich says,
"it is not the duty of the oppressed to educate the oppressor."[9] In naming white
people as an audience for this book, I do not intend to focus on whiteness in the
same way it is centered in our culture, but rather, in the words of writer Claudia

Rankine, with the awareness that "[w]hiteness is the problem, and whites are the ones who need to fix themselves. So you sort of need to center them."[10]

This book is based on over ten years of leading and co-leading The Bridge Project and over forty-five years of being a dancer. This book is not about virtue signaling or showing how "woke" I am. It's the confessional archive of an ongoing learning curve, a reckoning with privilege, and a writing without an end. This is a book that wrestles with the question of how, to paraphrase white author Jess Row, awareness of white privilege might become a way of life, a way of making art, and a way of being in the world.[11] Being an antiracist requires persistent self-awareness, constant self-criticism, and regular self-examination.[12] Because my whiteness creates blind spots in my perspective, my understanding of these issues will always be incomplete.

This book is a collection of questions tangled up in the process of shifting white cultural power. Asking questions about power imbalances and inequality can feel destabilizing and scary. But asking these questions is urgent. Feminist scholars like Ruth Frankenberg have written about how uncomfortable it is for white women in particular to name inequality and power imbalances. Rather than face these issues directly, white women have historically tended "to evade by means of partial description, euphemism, and self-contradiction those [issues] that [make] the speaker feel bad."[13] Sharing and giving away power is messy and difficult. In today's fraught call-out culture, it's tempting to want to hide our shortcomings and vulnerabilities. I write from inside imperfection as a way to normalize the fallibility of anti-racist work. In this book, I fight the legacy of white women's obfuscation of racial inequity by naming—in as direct, granular, and personal a way as possible—how these issues have played out in my relationships and work as an artist-curator.

In 2010, I started The Bridge Project as part of Hope Mohr Dance (HMD), the dance company that I founded in the San Francisco Bay Area in 2008. The Bridge Project is an interdisciplinary performing arts platform that approaches curating as a form of community organizing. I was motivated to start The Bridge Project by my desire to belong to a community of artists with a vibrant shared practice of critical thinking. I also wanted to experience artists' work that I knew would never be presented by bigger venues in the Bay Area. I wanted to see that work, I wanted other people in the Bay Area to see it, and I wanted us all to talk about it. I wanted to provide a broader historical and cultural context for contemporary artmaking. I wanted to invite others to consider where the field of dance has been, and I wanted us to ask: Where next?

The Bridge Project is artist-led. Working artists run it. The artists whom we support co-create program content with us. The Bridge Project has no brick-and-mortar facility and thus no obligation to a parent venue or institution. One upside of having no real estate is flexibility: we're able to partner with a wide variety of organizations and scale programs up or down in response to funding and artist needs. Another advantage of not having a building is that we have avoided the conflation of mission and venue that plagues so many arts organizations. The coronavirus has illuminated this risk: If an arts organization is forced to close their building, where does that leave their mission (and their budget)?

The downside of not having a building is that if we want to do a risky program, but we can't get buy-in from a partner venue, the program likely won't happen—we're usually dependent on financial subsidies from partner institutions. Like all arts organizations, we're constantly raising money to make programs possible.[14] However, the shift to virtual programming during the COVID-19 pandemic has freed us from reliance on partner venues.

The Bridge Project has developed iteratively over time in response to changing cultural and political contexts. What began as a feminist platform for shared dance programming has evolved into a multidisciplinary, intersectional[15] project with an explicit cultural and racial equity agenda. The program began with the intention of bridging the Bay Area and New York dance scenes. These early intentions have expanded to include building bridges between dance and other art forms and between artists and activists. In the past, audiences for my own choreography have been predominantly white. In contrast, audiences for The Bridge Project have been more diverse. As a result, The Bridge Project, as a social justice platform nested inside a white-founded dance company, bridges different audiences. The Bridge Project continues to shift as HMD transitions to a model of distributed leadership in order to implement equity values within the organization's structure.

This book captures a window in time from 2010–2020. It also captures a place: the San Francisco Bay Area. The Bridge Project's location in the Bay Area has allowed it more latitude to take experimental approaches to sacrosanct dance legacies than it if it were based in New York. In New York, the historical epicenter of dance power, dance artists and dance organizations work in the long shadow of Judson Church. Geographic distance from that postmodern legacy gives Bay Area artists a unique freedom to interrogate and disregard canon. In partnerships with The Bridge Project, both the Trisha Brown Dance Company (in 2016) and the Merce Cunningham Dance Company (in 2019) for the first time allowed dances to be transmitted for the explicit purpose of inspiring new works by artists who hailed from disciplines other than dance. I don't think these projects would have happened if we had proposed them in New York.

Rising economic inequality in the Bay Area and falling diversity in San Francisco inform everything that The Bridge Project does. As someone born in San Francisco in the early 1970s, I have witnessed how much diversity and culture the city has lost in the last fifty years. The city has a long history of activism and progressive politics.[16] But this reputation is now in question. Tech wealth, multiple waves of gentrification, rising housing costs, and the coronavirus have led to an exodus of artists, lower-income, and working-class people. Income inequality has risen dramatically in the Bay Area in the last few decades.[17] While the Bay Area as a region continues to become more diverse, San Francisco continues to get whiter.[18] Gentrification has disproportionately affected artists of color and their communities.[19]

This is the context in which The Bridge Project approaches curating as a form of community organizing. A thorough discussion of the history and practices of community organizing outside the arts context is beyond the scope of this book. Community organizing can use a variety of strategies, including collaboration, consensus, conflict, and pressure to build relationships, facilitate leadership, and create or recreate institutions to effect social change. When I refer to curating as a form of community organizing, I am not referring to old-school leftist approaches to organizing in the United States that can be traced back to Saul Alinsky's 1971 *Rules for Radicals*, which take a pragmatic approach to building grassroots political power by harnessing the self-interest of different stakeholders.[20] I am referring to more recent transformative approaches to organizing that focus not merely on concrete, short-term, and external political goals, but also on intersectional ideology, on sustainable, long-term social movements, and on personal, interpersonal, and organizational change.[21] When I frame curating as community organizing, I do so with the hope of imagining new models of relationship and support among artists and within arts organizations—models that transform our approach, rather than simply recast who holds power.

I also want to situate the work of shifting cultural power within the frame of "cultural strategy," a field of practice that centers artists, storytellers, media makers, and cultural influencers as agents of social change.[22] According to a report by Power California, cultural strategy takes a decolonial approach to culture. It aspires to transform "dominant cultural conditions" to become "conducive for all people to thrive and flourish."[23] Cultural strategy "centers the ways historically marginalized communities have maintained and transmitted their values."[24] The report lists three hallmarks of cultural strategy, with which I align curatorial practice:

- Deep engagement with artists and culture workers in envisioning and articulating a just future;
- Building and redistributing power for historically marginalized communities; and
- Creation of sustainable conditions for social change.[25]

In positioning curating within conversations about social change, I also situate curating in the "artivist" tradition. I use the term *artivism* to refer to cultural work as an ethical commitment and a tool for social change. Terms synonymous with artivism include "Art for Change,"[26] "public practice," "socially engaged art," and "social practice." Curating as community organizing means engaging on a daily basis with ongoing debates about artivism.

Artivism is not new. The term dates back at least to gatherings in the 1990s between Chicano artists from East Los Angeles and the Zapatistas in Chiapas, Mexico, and was further popularized through actions and artworks of East LA artists and musicians and at community art centers in LA.[27] Artivism, as defined by Chela Sandoval and Guisela Latorre, signifies "work created by individuals who see an organic relationship between art and activism."[28] Latorre writes that artivism "is both a strategy of survival and a necessary creative response to oppression."[29]

Artivism is often more about process than product. It is collaborative and participatory; the products of artivism often hold "equal or less importance to the collaborative act of creating them."[30] Along with an emphasis on audience participation, artivism is often concerned with the ethical and the everyday. Practitioners "freely blur the lines among object making, performance, political activism, community organizing, environmentalism and investigative journalism, creating a deeply participatory art."[31] M. K. Asante describes the process: "the artivist merges commitment to freedom and justice with the pen, the lens, the brush, the voice, the body, and the imagination."[32]

Artists from historically marginalized communities often have no choice but to intertwine their politics with their art. Their art is saturated with history by necessity because there is no possibility of living otherwise.[33] As Augusto

Boal, founder of Theater of the Oppressed in Brazil, said, "theater is political and politics is theater."[34] In contrast, for many white artists, integrating art-making and politics feels optional. In fact, there's a long tradition of white artists believing that they need to avoid race and politics in order to create.[35] Many white people don't need to think about racial identity; the term *identity* is rarely applied to whiteness:

> Racial identity is taken to be exclusive to people of color: When we speak about race, it is in connection with African Americans or Latinos or Asians or Native People or some other group that has been designated a minority. "White" is seen as the default, the absence of race.[36]

The aesthetic corollary of the whiteness-as-neutral fallacy is that white artists working in abstraction tend to take unity of form and content for granted.[37] White writer Hilarie M. Sheets quotes African American painter Jennie C. Jones, comparing herself to white visual artists Donald Judd and Fred Sandback:

> "Donald Judd didn't have to explain himself. Why do I have to?" asks Jennie C. Jones, an African American abstract painter who has grappled with the issue of how her work can or should reflect her race. Fred Sandback can make this beautiful line and not have to have it literally be a metaphor for his cultural identity.[38]

As African American visual artist Rashid Johnson says, "We would never ask Picasso why he painted white people."[39]

Filipino American choreographer Gerald Casel reflects on his experience responding to white choreographer Trisha Brown in The Bridge Project's 2016 project, *Ten Artists Respond to "Locus"*:

> [T]here is no such thing as pure movement for dancers of color. In my view, it is difficult to separate structural and systemic power from race. Among other intersectional factors (such as age, gender, class, etc.), dancing by brown and black bodies is read differently than dancing by white bodies. One of the assumptions that postmodern formalism arouses is that *any* body has the potential to be read as neutral—that there is such a thing as a universally unmarked body. As a dancer and choreographer of color, my body cannot be perceived as pure. My brown body cannot be read the same way as a white body, particularly in a white cube. This conflicted state rose to the surface during the workshops conducted around our learning the methodology of *Locus*. How was I to respond to this work without commenting on this

tension that I felt? How could I highlight the differences my body represented rather than ignoring or erasing them?[40]

Similarly, Taiwanese dancer and choreographer Peiling Kao reflects on her
experience performing *per[mute]ing,* her response to Trisha Brown in *Ten
Artists Respond to "Locus"*:

> No one seems have a problem seeing me as an Asian dancer when I do Euro-
> centric dance forms. Ironically, when I did Taiwanese/Chinese movement
> in *per[mute]ing,* viewers started seeking cultural meanings. An audience
> asked me if I was "trying to empower my Asian identity." But I have never
> thought of empowering my Taiwanese identity by using Taiwanese move-
> ment in my work. The audience's feedback led me to several questions: How
> do people assume and perceive the separation between Western and Eastern
> dance forms? Why do I need to do anything to "empower" my Taiwanese
> identity? Why does the doing of Taiwanese movement or speaking Taiwan-
> ese suddenly allow people to see me as Taiwanese? From my perspective, I am
> already a Taiwanese and nothing can change that. There is no need for
> empowerment.[41]

Whereas audiences often read the work of an artist of color as being about
their racial identity regardless of the artist's intentions, white artists have the
luxury of being able to choose to work in abstraction—to take their subjectivity out of their work.[42] African American visual artist Kara Walker, in a 2017
artist statement, expressed her fatigue from constantly having to explain her
work in terms of her racial identity, even as she acknowledged the inescapable
weight of American racial injustice:

> I don't really feel the need to write a statement about a painting show. I know
> what you all expect from me and I have complied up to a point. But frankly
> I am tired, tired of standing up, being counted, tired of 'having a voice' or
> worse 'being a role model.' Tired, true, of being a featured member of my
> racial group and/or my gender niche. It's too much, and I write this knowing
> full well that my right, my capacity to live in this Godforsaken country as a
> (proudly) raced and (urgently) gendered person is under threat by random
> groups of white (male) supremacist goons who flaunt a kind of patched
> together notion of race purity with flags and torches and impressive displays
> of perpetrator-as-victim sociopathy.[43]

White people should ask themselves, when going to see art by an artist of color,
if they expect the work to be about the artist's identity. Curator Kellie Jones says:

There's a story about Norman Lews's abstract expressionist colleagues telling him, *You need to make a lynching painting, man*. But in fact, if I put on my art history hat, for the most part, that was never African American artists' predominant mode—making art about violence—because they experienced it every day. It was more like art was a sacred, a fun, and a creative spot. Yes, you want to be part of a discourse that is antiracist, antiviolent, antihomophobic, whatever it is. But your art can also be about pleasure and love.[44]

One critique of artivism is that it conflates the ostensibly incompatible value systems of social justice and aesthetic excellence. For art critics like Shannon Jackson, social practice "brings to mind a series of other terms that do not always enjoy triumphant celebration: literal art, functionalist art, dumbed-down art, social realist art, victim art, consumable art, and related terms that have been coined to lament the capitulations to accessibility and intelligibility that can occur when art practice and social practice—aesthetics and politics—combine."[45] White critic Peter Schjeldahl, reviewing the 2019 Whitney Biennial, wrote of the "eternal futility of attempts to reconcile ethical right and wrong with aesthetic good and bad. These scales of value operate on different neural networks."[46] In 1994, white *New Yorker* critic Arlene Croce refused to review the premiere of Bill T. Jones' *Still/Here*, a dance about HIV/AIDS, arguing that its political content made it unreviewable.[47] A variant of this argument asserts that in artivism, aesthetics "have been reduced almost to zero."[48]

Not all critics of artivism are white. Some critics locate the problem not in artivism itself, but in the cultural context: when "all discourses have been politicized," an "anxious confusion of activism and criticism" results.[49] African American critic Wesley Morris says:

The goal is to protect and condemn work, not for its quality, per se, but for its values. Is this art or artist, this character, this joke bad for women, gays, trans people, nonwhites? Are the casts diverse enough? Is this museum show inclusive of enough different kinds of artists? Does the race of the curators correspond with the subject of the show or collection? Increasingly, these questions stand in for a discussion of the art itself. . . . It gives us culture whose artistic value has been replaced by moral judgment and leaves us with monocriticism. This might indeed be a kind of social justice. But it also robs us of what is messy and tense and chaotic and extrajudicial about art.[50]

Likewise, Latinx poet and curator manuel arturo abreu laments that social practice artworks "allow sociopolitical issues to be subsumed into aesthetic issues, such that a work can fail a community but still be considered good art."[51]

Perceived tensions between ethics and aesthetics raise issues not only for critics, but also for practitioners. At a forum for artists at Los Angeles Contemporary Exhibitions called *Pivoting*, the guiding question was: How can one mediate the social accountability connoted by ethics and the merits of self-derived aesthetics? Multidisciplinary artist and educator Dorit Cypis, who moderated the panel, described the dynamic: "When you talk about a form like public practice, when you weigh the content of the public into your work, as part of the generative materials of your own practice, I think that brings up a lot of questions about ethics."[32] That inquiry can result in what artist Amitis Motevalli called at that event "the collision of ethics and aesthetics."[33]

I've experienced these tensions on a personal level. Throughout HMD's shift to an equity-driven model of distributed leadership, colleagues, mentors, friends, and supporters have voiced concerns that a focus on politics will come at the expense of my identity as an artist. "What happened to your art practice? I feel a sense of loss," said one white donor, who began supporting HMD because she was drawn to my choreography. This book challenges the assumption that art and politics are a zero-sum game.

In the context of dance and performance, it's important to distinguish the values of artivism from those of postmodernism. Since Judson Dance Theater in the 1960s, postmodern choreographers have democratized the vocabulary of dance by using task-based and pedestrian movement.[54] Yvonne Rainer refused mastery and virtuosity in her influential "No Manifesto;" the story of the Judson Dance Theater artist cohort can be seen as "one of mutual refusal."[55] But however much these postmodern refusals and their progeny democratized dance vocabulary, they did not democratize the dance field itself. Judson can be seen as political in that it laid some of the groundwork for subsequent experiments in dismantling dominant cultural narratives.[56] But in general, postmodernism's egalitarian urges have been relegated to issues of form. The postmodern aesthetic in itself has not shifted power dynamics in the field nor in society. In contrast, artivism looks beyond form to change the power relations of the world at large. Today, socially engaged postmodern choreographers must reconcile what at times can feel like the competing priorities of these two radical traditions.

Another critique of artivism attacks its democratic impulse. Some question why artivism assumes collaboration is a good in itself. White curator Hans Obrist asks: "Collaboration is the answer, but what is the question?"[57] Others wonder if collaboration is compatible with rigorous authorship. Some choreographers feel that too much democracy is not good for art. White art critic

Hal Foster suggests that artivism has arisen as a form of substitute democratic participation: "Perhaps discursivity and sociability are in the foreground of art today because they are scarce elsewhere."[38] Foster asserts that artivism is a "pale, part-time substitute" for real engagement in the actual democratic process.[59] He frames artivism as a form of faux politics lacking the rigor and power to "evoke a democratic community" or "predict an egalitarian world."[60] This critique echoes one raised by those who urge the nonprofit social service sector not to abandon more radical agendas in lieu of providing basic direct services, thereby becoming a "shadow state" instead of a force for social transformation.[61] These critiques ask: Why should government failures compromise artistic or activist visions?

There is no one way to participate in democracy. Civic engagement can take many forms, from voting to dancing, and all of these forms have the potential to contribute to political consciousness, enliven public dialogue, and activate the power of the people. Along this spectrum of engagement, some artists see participation in traditional electoral politics as a natural manifestation of their artistic practice. "Legislative theater" takes Augusto Boal's interactive theater exercises from the stage into the real world as a tool for proposing policy change.[62] In 2017, the "Artist Campaign School" was founded to train artists to run for public office with the belief that artists, as experts in creative problem-solving, are uniquely situated to catalyze social change.[63] 4Culture in King County, Washington brings artists into government by matching them with policymakers as consultants on specific issues.[64] And yet art is not simply a gateway to "legitimate" political engagement. It is its own sui generis form of politics.

The collapse of art and activism into each other accelerated in reaction to the racist, sexist, ableist, xenophobic, and homophobic rhetoric and policies of the Trump Administration. In the San Francisco Bay Area, where artists have been acutely feeling the insidious impacts of gentrification for many years, there is an added urgency to conversations around socially engaged art. The exodus of artists from San Francisco, coupled with the loss of nonprofit arts spaces, threatens to create, as Chicano performance artist Guillermo Gómez-Peña laments, "a world of unbearable sameness."[65] For those who remain, a logic of scarcity threatens to overshadow art practice. As a curatorial colleague said, explaining her decision to leave the Bay Area, "I want to be someplace where the prevailing topic of conversation among artists is not how hard it is to survive." In this charged environment, cultural equity has become the dominant lens through which artists, curators, and funders make and evaluate work in the Bay Area.

In order to shift cultural power, white artists and curators must reckon with how white privilege informs our approach to socially engaged art. If we critique artivism, how might our critiques be, in the words of manuel arturo abreu, "steeped in whiteness"?[66] When do we categorize or dismiss art as "socially engaged" or political as a way of viewing, making, and evaluating art that we see as something other than "pure" form? How does whiteness inform our visions and models of what community, public engagement, dialogue, and performance can and should look like?

With this context and holding these questions, this book reflects on the following elements of curating as community organizing:

- Shifting cultural power through transparency, artist leadership, and distributed leadership (Chapter 2)
- Creating an artist commons (Chapter 3)
- Inviting difficult conversations (Chapter 4)
- Facilitating hybrid forms (Chapter 5)
- Expanding the canon (Chapter 6)
- Reckoning with aesthetics (Chapter 7)

When we reckon with and decenter whiteness, we open imaginative space for more equitable models of artmaking and art community. We create possibilities for shifting cultural power.

Chapter 2

Shifting Cultural Power through Transparency, Artist Power, and Distributed Leadership

TRANSPARENCY

Curating as community organizing requires that artists and curators be transparent about their values, biases, and motives. As curator Michèle Steinwald advocates, "accountability is critical" if we are to move the dance field toward equity.[67] What are our priorities? What are our privileges? Steinwald notes that if we are transparent about our motives, others can hold us accountable if our work falls short of our stated ideals.[68] As Steinwald points out, building accountability must happen not only in relationship to performance; it must begin in the studio, with our physical practices:

> There's this nostalgic sense in dance that you go into a studio, you feel inspired, your body moves a certain way, you translate it to a cast and then you manipulate it into choreography—that it's an instinctual process that happens through inspiration, so it transcends language and one's ability to explain their motives. I don't ascribe to that. Explanation of the motives that inform choreography is just an exercise we haven't done.[69]

In working with artists, especially artists from communities different than my own, disclosing my personal motives is essential to building trust. Artists of color have ample reasons to distrust white curators and artistic directors: long histories of exploitation, tokenism, and appropriation. As white people in the arts, we cannot assume that artists of color are partnering with us out of trust. We must earn their trust. With this in mind, before digging into case studies involving other artists, I'll begin with transparency about my own story.

I'm a white, bisexual, cis-female born in 1971. I'm swimming in privilege: I'm highly educated, a US citizen, able-bodied, and have been financially comfortable my entire life. My ancestors were not all as lucky. I come from German Jewish immigrants on my father's side, some of whom died in the Holocaust. On my mother's side of the family are generations of farmers descended from English immigrants. There is not a history of dancing in my family. Nor is there a history of activism. There is a pattern in my family of unrealized female potential—women renouncing their path in order to accommodate men.

I felt called to dance as a young child and began taking ballet when I was four. Fourteen years later, I became a feminist. My experience of coming to feminist consciousness was sudden and revelatory. In the fall of 1990, during my first year of college, I went to hear the great poet Adrienne Rich, a lesbian feminist who wrote extensively about the possibilities that sit at the intersection of politics and poetry. I went into a packed church with private rage and sadness; when I was eleven, my parents separated and we moved abruptly, which sent me down a path of depression and self-destructive behavior. I went into that church feeling alone. I came out with an awareness that my struggles were related to those of other women. Suddenly, I had a new vocabulary, a new tribe, and a new sense of voice. Suddenly, I understood that, despite having trained as a dancer for my entire life, my body was not entirely my own. Male privilege and male power impacted how my body was allowed to move and be seen. I now had both a dancing body and a politicized body. Could these two bodies be in conversation?

I've held that question ever since. After hearing Rich, I started working in a domestic violence clinic. I went to *Take Back the Night* marches and Pro Choice marches. I changed the course of my studies to Latin American Studies with a focus on women's movements in revolutionary contexts. I wrote my undergraduate thesis on the domestic violence movement in Nicaragua because I was interested in the "private" side of that country's tumultuous transition to democracy. Feminism felt, and continues to feel, as urgent as dancing.

Work in the women's movement led me into other kinds of activism, including advocacy on behalf of immigrant rights and community gardening in low-income neighborhoods. I led delegations of North American health care workers to Nicaragua and led an AmeriCorps community gardening team in South Central LA. These experiences showed me the extent of my white privilege. I started to learn how to listen to people of color.

I remember vividly the day the O. J. Simpson verdict came down in 1995. My community gardening team, all African American except for me, took a break to watch the verdict on TV. We were sitting in a community room in a housing project in South Central LA with about fifty other people. I was one of two white people. When the not guilty verdict was announced, the room erupted in cheers. Everyone was hugging and high-fiving. My eyes met the other white person across the room. We both sat in stunned silence. I felt my whiteness acutely. I felt the blindnesses of white feminism. In hindsight, I see that I was feeling the "same overwhelming sensation of hopelessness and discouragement that Black people feel all too many times."[70]

Wanting to make a bigger impact as an activist, I went law school. I took three leaves of absence from law school to dance professionally for various choreographers, including Lucinda Childs, Liz Gerring, Pat Catterson, and Douglas Dunn—all white postmodern choreographers in the Cunningham and Judson Dance Theater lineage. As I was finishing law school, I was offered a job with the Trisha Brown Dance Company.

Until the time I took the job with Trisha Brown, I lived a double life. I worked in public interest law jobs where I wouldn't talk about being a dancer, lest people not take me seriously as a lawyer. For the same reason, I wouldn't tell people in the dance world that I was in law school. (Years later, I took a stand against this dualism by calling my blog "the body is the brain.") This schism was at times stimulating. I enjoyed interacting with people who spoke different codes and had different priorities. But after many years of this balancing act, I felt its toll on my inner life. Also, I had the rest of my life to be an advocate, but my prime dancing years were short.

I took the job with Trisha Brown. In doing so, I left advocacy behind. I was "just" a dancer. I enjoyed being a vehicle for Trisha's brilliant aesthetic. It was a joy to be able to hone my somatic intelligence on a granular level.

After many years, I felt finished with being someone else's dancer and done with living in New York. I returned to the Bay Area to focus on my own work.

My first project was *Under the skin*, a dance inspired by teaching creative movement to breast cancer survivors. The cast featured both professional dancers and breast cancer survivors telling personal stories through movement, text, and voiceover. The next project I directed was *The Unsayable*, which featured a mixed cast of professional dancers and military veterans exploring personal story through movement and text, inspired by teaching creative movement in the Homeless Veterans Unit of the Palo Alto Veterans Affairs Hospital. Each of these projects took two years from initial community engagement to performance.

Choreographer Paloma McGregor has said that every dance is a "community-based dance" and that often, that term is a euphemism for a dance made with low-income people, people who are not professional dancers, or performers of color.[71] With this in mind, I don't call these early projects "community-based." A more accurate description is that these dances involved people from communities that were not my own.

Here's an excerpt from my program notes from *The Unsayable*:

> In the words of Joyce Carol Oates (writing in response to Arlene Croce's refusal to review Bill T. Jones' *Still/Here*, his 1994 dance about people with HIV/AIDS), "there is a long and honorable tradition of art that bears witness to human suffering." Cognizant of this lineage, and having facilitated a similar project in 2007 with breast cancer survivors, I entered the year-long process of *The Unsayable*: six months of development and outreach, three months of workshop, and a mere two months of rehearsal. What you see tonight is first and foremost the culmination of a group emotional process honoring veterans' voices. Second, it is a work of choreography. Balancing the two has been a fascinating challenge. The project's fundamental premise has been to engage veterans not as mere source material, but as artistic collaborators in conversation with dancers. I hope the work imparts a deeper understanding of what it means to bear witness and what it means to be a citizen. The veterans were not selected for the content of their stories. This is the first time they have ever performed professionally on stage.[72]

Noble intentions drove these projects. They were positive, transformative experiences for the performers. I remain close with many of them over a decade later.

But I felt that these dances were not good art. At the time, I found it hard to reconcile a white postmodern aesthetic with the need to honor participant voices. I felt that in order to integrate "non-dancer" participants into the choreography, I needed to limit the mixed ensemble's vocabulary to simple pedestrian gestures. On the other hand, if I wanted more choreographic complexity, the "non-dancer" performers were marginalized (standing, sitting, or watching). Powerful moments could be found by juxtaposing simple gesture and complex dancing, but often, the choice was between a limited vocabulary and a fractured ensemble. We spent much time in the creative process on the simple rules of performance (for example, don't scratch an itch onstage). And most significantly, for victims of trauma, performance can be a powerful trigger. Mediating trauma, supporting mental health, and processing intense group dynamics consumed energy that might otherwise have been focused on craft. In these ways, I found that rooting the artmaking process in the raw material of trauma threatened to diminish the art itself. As a young choreographer steeped in white classical and modern dance, I could only see craft as a practice of shutting other voices out, rather than letting them in.

These early projects led me to question my own choreographic intentions and the intentions behind socially engaged performance in general. I left these projects unsure how dancemaking could simultaneously prioritize participant healing, raise awareness of social issues, and be well crafted. Would a workshop behind closed doors be a better context for expressing trauma? Would other forums be more appropriate for advocacy?

These early attempts at making issue-driven performance also sensitized me to the tendency, in so many socially engaged dances, to rely on projections and voiceover to hold the political content of the work. In many overtly political dances, if you remove the projection and voiceover, the work could be a generic dance about anything. The politics remain on the surface. Too often, as in my case, the artist doesn't allow the politics to permeate their choreographic thinking. Put another way, the subject matter overwhelms the authorship. This can happen because of a desire to make the work accessible, deference to collaborators, a weak artistic voice, or a narrow artistic palette. For whatever reason, the exchange between the outside world and the artist's inner life does not go deeply enough. The dancing is regurgitated from other sources, rather than the result of embodied research that metabolizes the source material through the body. Adrienne Rich wrote that many poems "full of liberal or radical hope and outrage fail to lift off the ground, for which 'politics' is blamed rather than a failure of poetic nerve."[73] When a socially engaged dance fails to "lift off the ground," we must ask whether the choreographer lacked poetic nerve, rather than blame the genre of socially engaged art.

My early artivist projects were accountable to the communities they served. They were accountable to my activist goals. But they weren't accountable to me as an artist. I did not know how to honor other people's stories without my own voice leaving the building. I was not transparent with everyone in the process about my needs as an artist. I wasn't even transparent with myself. Asking for what you need as an artist can be challenging, especially if you are making performance that is not based on your own story. Only now, more than a decade later, do I feel equipped to balance collaboration and my own voice. I got to this point because I emerged from these early performance projects knowing that I needed to find my poetic nerve. I needed permission for my unconscious to take the work off-message. I needed the freedom to go into the studio without being held accountable to anyone's story—even my own—about what the work was supposed to be about. I wanted to make art that retained some mystery. I needed to figure out how to make the kind of art I wanted to make *and* challenge the status quo.

And so, for many years as a choreographer, I moved away from telling other people's stories so that I could hear my own. At the same time, I decided to put my political energies into curating and supporting other artists. The Bridge Project was born. I felt like I needed to put a fence around my own art in order to listen within. In doing so, I exercised my privilege, as a white artist, to tell myself that I was insulating my art practice from politics. I now see that you can never insulate yourself from politics; the act of trying to do so is in itself political. Awareness of my privilege, in this and other respects, continues to drive my curatorial practice.

ARTIST POWER

Empowering artists empowers communities. Curators must make space for artists to step into power. Decentering myself and its corollary, letting other artists lead, has been a central learning space for me and perhaps my most valuable curatorial strategy. As someone who has long invoked the adage, "If you want something right, do it yourself," decentering myself is not always my default approach. But increasingly, it has become my central curatorial commitment.

White people sometimes use decentering to justify their retreat from difficult conversations. I'm interested in practicing decentering not as a way to hide, but as a way of holding space for others while remaining engaged and accountable. It's crucial that we not use decentering whiteness as a way of bringing people of color into toxic structures. I don't want to make, as Tomi Obaro writes, "a few token hires who are placed into the same system, forced to do all the hard work of undoing years of systemic harm, and eventually burn out and leave the [arts] altogether, thoroughly disillusioned."[74] Obaro continues: "What about a justice that is more radical, more forward-looking, one that does not perpetuate existing power structures with a slightly browner tinge?"[75] Let's decenter whiteness to make space for new models.

For white artists, decentering the self may mean, when handed a performance opportunity or a grant, considering offering that opportunity to an artist of color. It may mean sitting out a grant cycle. It may mean declining an award or a nomination. Gerald Casel, an artist commissioned by The Bridge Project in 2016 in *Ten Artists Respond to "Locus,"* and also the 2019 Community Engagement Residency lead artist behind *Dancing Around Race*, writes: "White choreographers need to move back and make space. If you don't see your privilege or your access, because you're taking up that space or position, then someone else is unable to occupy it."[76]

For white artist-curators, decentering the self means curating programs that are not tied to our own work, lineage, or ego. This means supporting artists not because they want to work with me or because they're in my circle, but because their work is necessary and in need of support. Decentering the curator means making space for artists to self-determine their process and terms of production. When a white curator is presenting an artist of color, having the artist lead can be "an act of reversal whereby the colonized takes control of his/her own representation, thus disrupting some of the power dynamics of objectification."[77] Examples of letting artists control the process of cultural production can include: booking and paying for an artist's studio space or public event but not attending unless invited; if invited, not talking much, mostly listening; facilitating a situation in which an artist can decide what they want to do with resources and when they want to get paid; reminding an artist that they can change their mind about the course of work midway through the project; letting an artist decide whether an event will be open to the general public or to specific affinity groups only; inviting an artist to write marketing copy for their event; supporting an artist's decisions about the format and duration of a post-show discussion.

For white curators, shifting cultural power means curating artists of color in a way that advances the artist, not the presenting organization. Artists know the difference. As David Herrera, lead artist in the 2019–2020 Community Engagement Residency, *LatinXtensions*, said to me:

> When you say that the curating work is not about you, that feels different than when somebody says, "I'd like to give you $1,000," but then they use my

work to secure a much larger grant. It can start to feel like, wait, did I just get used by this organization to get a much bigger grant for themselves? And I'm getting a tiny fraction of that? In the end, an organization claiming to help artists of color ends up helping themselves more than they are helping the people that they're claiming to help. It's different when an organization is actually interested in pushing somebody upward with little interest in making it about their organization. I'm used to questioning someone's motives when there's money involved.[78]

In a funding landscape that increasingly wants to fund artists of color, many white-led cultural organizations, including HMD, have repositioned themselves as regranting organizations. But writing checks to artists of color does not shift cultural power. The regranting paradigm allows existing white-led organizations to maintain control over resources and relationships with funders. White curators and cultural leaders must go beyond the regranting model and connect artists of color directly with funders. We must also evolve our organizational models to give artists of color a seat at the table with real power over aesthetics and resources.

Being a regranting organization, especially if the organization is white-led and regrants to artists of color, can be problematic because it leaves the organization in control of resources and access to funders. To build trust, total financial transparency is crucial regarding grant amounts awarded, budgets submitted by the organization to funders, the terms of the grant, and the timing of disbursements to both the organization and the artist.[79] To combat the inequities inherent in the regranting relationship, arts organizations must find ways to facilitate direct access to resources to artists without playing a gatekeeping role. Funders must also play a part in shifting power to artists by allowing fiscally sponsored artists to apply directly for opportunities, not just through intermediary organizations with tax-exempt status. Sometimes, even when program officers inside arts funding institutions push for reforms to empower individual artists, larger structural issues still favor the power of larger and white-led regranting organizations.[80]

COVID-19 triggered a wave of cancellations in which artists were too frequently unpaid for promised work, thereby underscoring power imbalances in the field between individual artists and arts organizations. "Creating New Futures," a working group born out of the pandemic, is developing recommendations and contractual templates for dance and performance artists, organizers, and nonprofit institutions to support more equitable conditions for artists.[81]

The "Creating New Futures" working document states: "Our systems weren't working, and we all knew it. They are unsustainable and we know it. They are inequitable and we know it. They rely on a scarcity mentality and the freelance labor of artists working with no safety net. It is time for radical change."[82]

We must empower artists not only through public programs, but also through organizational models. As I discuss below, we must implement distributed leadership models that democratize decisions and give artists power over resources and aesthetics. In this way, communities, not organizations, can directly give voice to their own needs.

DISTRIBUTED LEADERSHIP

Shifting cultural power implicates both public-facing programs and internal organizational structures. Often there is a disconnect between the two. This disconnect can show up in many ways: program staff may be ahead of a Board of Directors in terms of their commitment to cultural equity; the demographics of the staff or the Board may not reflect the artists that an organization serves; an artistic director may employ a collaborative ethos in the studio, while organizational decisions remain top-down. All of these schisms suggest that the organization has work to do to value-align their internal structures with a commitment to cultural equity. An organization may claim to be in solidarity with artists of color, but cultural power will only shift when historically white-led arts organizations democratize the way decisions get made inside the organization. Do artists and artists of color have a seat at the table? Often, arts organizations run on hierarchical models by default: people are unaware that there are alternatives. But regardless of an organization's business model and tax status, implementing equity-driven best practices and democratic governance is possible.[83]

One strategy for shifting power within existing cultural organizations is for white people to reposition themselves and distribute leadership. A commitment to cultural equity is not the only possible motivating force behind a move to distributed leadership; the shift may be forced when a founder moves or dies or a short-term strategy. There are clear benefits to distributed leadership models, including:

- Maximizing creativity by opening up space for everyone's self-expression;
- Increasing staff ownership over the work;
- Preventing founder burnout and creating a more sustainable organization by locating energy in multiple people;

– Building trust and relationships with a wider community; and
– Creating opportunities for learning and change within the organization.

Beyond these considerations, HMD's decision to move to a model of distributed leadership was a moral imperative inextricably bound up in our commitment to cultural and racial equity. According to the "Continuum of Becoming an Anti-Racist Organization," a "commitment to institutional restructuring" is an essential step in becoming a "Fully Inclusive Anti-Racist Multicultural Organization in a Transformed Society."[84]

Repositioning, unlike diversity, asks white people to give up power. It thus comes as no surprise that the "arts sector is entrenched in a diversity (instead of an equitable outcomes) framework."[85] Nonprofit administrator Cyndi Suarez writes that the concept of diversity "flows from a supremacist perspective. It is framed as a value to the dominant. It adds nuance to a situation, but it does not change the relationships of power."[86]

Cultural equity requires a deeper commitment than the one-off opportunities and optics that come with diversity. It requires a long-term, activist commitment to change power structures. To expand upon Ibram X. Kendi's statement that "if a person has no record of power or policy change, then that person is not an activist," there is no such thing as a race-neutral dance organization; every dance organization is producing either racial inequity or equity.[87] To produce equity, we need to go beyond diversity. White curators and artistic directors need to give up power. Curator Michèle Steinwald states:

> People in institutions trade in expertise and hierarchy. By dismantling that, they have to reposition their place in the system. Not everybody's willing to do that. That is the decolonizing: the replacing of patterns that I may not have full control over and cognizance of with patterns that are aligned with my values and my goals.[88]

This is lifelong work that cannot be accomplished passively. "Compassion is an unstable emotion," wrote Susan Sontag. "It needs to be translated into action, or it withers."[89]

Within existing arts organizations that have historically been hierarchical, white curators and directors can reposition themselves by moving the organization to a model of shared leadership wherein they enable the "conditions for distributed leadership to thrive."[90] Distributed leadership models are dynamic, emergent, and unique to each organization.[91] In models of distributed leadership, directors and curators must demonstrate what is called "flexible adjustment": leading from the front when required and stepping back when required to allow those with historically less authority the opportunity to lead.[92]

During the writing of this book, HMD transitioned to a model of distributed leadership in which we changed from a white founder-led hierarchy to a multiracial, multiethnic co-directorship that I share with two other staff: Karla Quintero and Cherie Hill, both female artists of color. For me, distributing leadership was the only way the organization could align our internal structures with the values that drive our public programs.

When it is value-driven, distributed leadership must be more than moving items from the founder or director's "to do" list onto someone else's. It must be more than cosmetic or perfunctory title changes. For HMD, the shift to distributed leadership has so far involved all of the following:

- Moving to a co-curatorial model for all of The Bridge Project's programs;
- Transitioning to a Board of 100% working artists so that the Board reflects the people we support;
- Working with an equity-driven consulting group to help us navigate the power shift mindfully and show us our blind spots;
- An intensive internal learning and listening campaign in which we met with other nonprofit leaders navigating similar shifts in leadership;
- A series of community meetings about what distributed leadership model could and should look like (with all participating artists paid for their participation);
- Implementing pay equity by moving the founder/Artistic Director from salary to hourly pay and paying all three co-directors the same hourly rate;
- Revising our statement of values and operating principles, our by-laws, and Board Prospectus to reflect our values;
- The white founder stepping back from selecting artists for our residency program and turning over the selection process to artists who had done the program in the past, along with staff of color;
- Implementing a paid artist curatorial council;
- Meeting with funders as a team to shift those crucial relationships out of founder exclusive control.

As I write this book, we continue to discuss further structural changes that will decenter whiteness and bring artists into positions of power over resources and aesthetics within the organization.

Beyond structural changes, distributed leadership must be a shift in organizational culture—a change in how work actually gets done. As Cyndi Suarez writes:

> Oftentimes leaders or social-change activists think that, if they create and implement new structures, they can shift the way people in an organization interact. Focusing instead on creating collective understanding of how people are currently interacting and their desired ways of interacting can lead to exponential and immediate change.[93]

Below are some of the ways, which I discuss further below, in which an organization's internal culture must shift in order for distributed leadership to be meaningful.

- Certainty → Uncertainty
- Culture of efficiency → Culture of democracy
- Action-oriented → Process-oriented
- Founder/Director time → Multiple approaches to time welcome
- Cult(ure) of personality → Culture of community
- Culture of control → Culture of trust
- Fixed roles → Fluid roles
- Diversity mindset → Equity mindset
- "People of color are who we serve" → "How can we give power to people of color?"
- Regranting/Gatekeeping resources → Facilitating direct artist access to resources

Shifting to a model of distributed leadership is time-consuming, slow, and expensive. It floods the organization with uncertainty: What's my role in this meeting? Will the organization lose its funding? Who do we serve now? Organizational transformation requires letting go of the status quo. Often, especially in times of crisis, leaders can hunker down and prioritize organizational survival above all else. This logic of scarcity works against the acceptance of uncertainty that shifting leadership models requires.

One of the biggest shifts in organizational culture associated with distributing leadership relates to how the organization handles time. For over ten years, I ran HMD prioritizing efficiency, perfection, and quick response. In some ways, this approach served the organization well: we have a strong record of securing grants and opportunities. But as cultural and racial equity became a priority, this approach no longer reflected organizational values. Now, instead of responding immediately to an email, I need to wait. I need to let someone else respond or I need to bring other people into the decision. In either case, organizational response time is slower. Within distributed leadership, individuals can still have specialized skill sets and distinct spheres of responsibility. A flat organizational structure does not mean that every single decision must be consensus-based. But an ensemble makes decisions more slowly than a soloist. Democratic process takes more time than fiat.

Moving to pay equity can further impact how founders relate to time. When HMD moved to a distributed leadership, I moved from salary to hourly pay in order to implement pay equity among staff. In doing so, I began tracking my hours for the first time since founding the company. For years, I worked constantly with no idea how many hours I put into the organization. Like so many other founders in the arts, the organization was my "baby" and was inextricably wrapped up in my personality. When the organization experienced success or setback, I took it personally. The concrete step of tracking my time helped me build a boundary between personal life and work. Now I set limits on my hours. Tracking my time also translates the work into discrete, tangible tasks (for example, I now know that I spent a certain number of hours a month on artist contracts), which in turn makes it easier to delegate the work to others.

Distributed leadership challenges the cult of personality so common in the arts. What are the implications for choreographic practice? Historically, the single choreographer vision has been the model for making and promoting dance in western culture. (Although many choreographers work collaboratively, dance is often less collaborative than it looks.) But under a model of distributed leadership, the question is, "What can we do together?" rather than "What is my vision and how can you implement it?"

Dance organizations often begin anchored in the work of a choreographer and expand into additional programs associated with a school, theater, residency, or mentorship program. How do power dynamics in the anchoring dance company translate into other program areas? There is a trend of white artists creating organizations to serve their own work and then branching out into social justice-driven public programming. Are these programmatic attempts at offsetting white founder footprint enough? In the studio environment, control over authorship has different stakes than in the curatorial decisions of a theater or the pedagogical decisions of a school. How might distributed leadership manifest differently in these different realms? Is it necessary to disentangle public programs from the founding choreographer's artistic work in order for the organization to evolve? Does committing to distributed leadership as a curator mean that I need to resign my position as choreographer?

These questions have been the trickiest for me in the work of distributing leadership. They touch on my identity as an artist. They implicate financial viability (does the organization's financial future rest in my voice as an artist or in work that serves a broader community or social movement?). These shifts can also be confusing for donors and patrons. In response to a survey that we sent out regarding our shift to distributed leadership, one respondent asked: "I always thought HMD's purpose was to be a place for Hope to express her artistic vision. Does Hope have to give up her vision in order to repair inequities?" For me, this question misses the point. What if repairing inequities is part of my vision as an artist?

Part of this work is communicating its complexity to the community. Power is both felt and perceived. Although staff may make a shift to sharing power, it may take a long time for funders to stop assuming that they should call the founder first. If the organization carries the founder or artistic director's name, this fact alone is an obstacle to the community believing that the organization operates on a model of distributed leadership. Even in telling the story of distributed leadership, it's important to distribute who controls the narrative. White people need to make space for those stepping into power to shape, share, and own the organization's story.

Distributed leadership is a shift from a culture of control to a culture of trust. As a founder, I have deeply ingrained habits of initiation. For years, I unilaterally made the agenda for every meeting. If I had an idea, I often implemented it without consulting anyone. I worried that anyone who worked for me wouldn't get it "right." Choreographer and curator Bhumi B. Patel, HMD's former Program Coordinator and now Board member, recalls that when she worked for me, "Often in my work it felt like there was a magnifying glass on me. The feeling of second-guessing myself didn't feel good. It didn't necessarily feel like a thing I knew how to bring up, particularly given the power dynamic and structure."[94] Our working relationship illuminated the costs of my need to micromanage. It's easy for white liberals to endorse racial equity as an abstract ideal. It's harder when you need to let someone else decide how to word a grant proposal. Alicia Garza, founder of Black Lives Matter, said, "I can't have white supervisors anymore. It's too much. I'm being micromanaged."[95] What good is power if not joined with time, space, and trust?

Shifting power is a layered process. Even after HMD had announced our shift to a model of distributed leadership, I still caught myself making unilateral decisions in areas where, as a staff, we had agreed that decisions would be made collectively. Sharing input is only the beginning. Who has powers of implementation? Who holds the big picture of the organization's financial capacity? Who has access to budgets? Who has the authority to sign contracts with artists? Who writes the checks?

Another organizational culture shift related to distributing leadership is recognizing the assumption that often exists within arts organizations that people of color are merely people whom the organization "serves." This assumption, common in language that white-led and regranting organizations use in funding applications, positions people of color in the passive, subservient role of receiving help. This assumption denies agency to people of color and ignores that many people of color are cultural leaders.[96]

In addition to directors stepping back, distributed leadership involves staff stepping up into power. Both shifts require people to rethink their capacity, agency, and relationship to the organization. Do staff have the time, interest, and bandwidth to assume positions of expanded power? Founders must give people stepping up time and space to envision the future of the organization. And founders must explicitly value the contributions of people stepping into power. Karla Quintero began working for HMD as a dancer and now, through our move to distributed leadership, is one of The Bridge Project three co-curators. She reflects on this process:

> Can a shift to distributed leadership within a nonprofit arts organization support the dismantling of ways of working that perpetuate inequity, logics of scarcity, and racism? My work towards realizing a model for distributed leadership within HMD is an invitation to explore this question with an open heart and an open mind. I began working with HMD as an administrative manager in June 2017. My role shifted in 2018 to Director of Marketing and Development and most recently in 2020 to Co-Director of The Bridge Project, a role I share with Cherie Hill and Hope Mohr. Our sharing of leadership around the visioning and implementation for the 2020 Bridge

Project *Power Shift: Improvisation, Activism, and Community* has prompted many positive changes, including pay equity and increased financial transparency among staff. Within HMD's programming, this shift is resulting in a growing emphasis on community-building and dialogue as artistic practice.

For HMD, this process is iterative. Each change reveals another opportunity for creating a more equitable balance of power within the organization and so forth. In dialogue with artists we partner with, we are exploring how far these changes can go. I am particularly intrigued by the contradiction of moving towards collective leadership within a predominantly individualistic, and hyper-capitalist culture. I'm excited to share what we learn and unlearn with the field.[97]

Cherie Hill, HMD's Director of Art in Community, reflects on these shifts as well:

In stepping back as a founder, Hope has adopted similar practices to what Karla and I perform as employees. She is tracking her hours to work part-time, comparable to ours, and we all receive the same hourly wage. I see these actions as a vital start to decreasing hierarchy. As far as power and decision-making, I am still learning how that emerges within my position. I believe what stepping up and making decisions means will become more apparent as our work progresses. I predict that as our work continues, and we have more time together as a team, more clarity around who holds power, when they execute, or the adoption of specific decision-making structures will emerge.

I feel honored to be a part of this distributive leadership process because I believe that creating different structures for nonprofit art organizations is imperative for the future. The traditional model of a founder or executive director at the head continues to be problematic concerning community efforts around inclusion and equity. I hope that as the three of us co-create a distributive leadership model for HMD, other nonprofit organizations are inspired to follow.[98]

Examples of distributed leadership abound in the dance and performance world. Danspace Project in New York has the artist-curated *Platform* and *Food for Thought* series; Movement Research in New York has several rotating guest curatorial teams for their festivals. Codirectorship as a model is on the rise, even at large, traditional arts organizations like New York City Ballet. Cal Shakes, a theater organization in Berkeley, California, introduced a "programming matrix" that allowed its entire staff to have input on the plays they wanted the organization to produce and to weigh in on considerations like alignment with a commitment to diversity, equity, and inclusion:

> The matrix provided a place for staff to go to bat for a play they felt passionate about.... From this input, the artistic director could work more collaboratively with the managing director and board of directors to make final decisions on the season's programming... these leaders made decisions they wouldn't have otherwise made without collaborative engagement with staff.[99]

Collaborative, cooperative, collective, and rotating leadership structures have the potential to shift power to artists and decenter whiteness. Collectives like AUNTS, which began in New York, and Salta and the QTBIPOC Performing Artist Hive, both based in the Bay Area, have been collective since their inception. The Hive, a project of artists Estrellx Supernova (formerly known as randy reyes) and Daria Garina, was developed during their 2019 Community Engagement Residency. The Hive's artist statement reads in part:

> We acknowledge that the intelligence and strength of our collective are greater than any one of its parts and those attributes come from alchemizing our respective gifts through and beyond the intersections of our differences / ancestral lineages. We gather and from there see what wants to happen.[100]

Beyond repositioning, as white curators we must also ask: When is it time for an arts organization to cease to exist? Like some monuments, many arts organizations are born to serve a particular person, time, or place. Like some monuments, arts organizations may at some point cease to be relevant and useful. We must make peace with the ephemerality of dance organizations just as we make peace with the ephemerality of dance itself. Allowing some organizations to die is crucial for the health of the field.

Repositioning for white curators and directors may mean leaving the organization altogether. At the Leeway Foundation in Philadelphia, a white founder stepped away from her role entirely to hand power over to a community council in order to implement a mission of "supporting women and trans artists and cultural producers working in communities at the intersection of art, culture, and social change."[101] In 2020, New York performance venue PSNY announced that it would be turning over the keys to the building to a group of artists for a year:

For the year of 2020 a group of NYC-based artists and collectives have been given the mandate to run the organization together with our staff, board, and leadership. The artists have received keys to the spaces, have moved into our business offices, and will move into our theaters next month. They have full transparency into the organization's inner workings and full artistic control of our programming including oversight of the website. Our total annual production budget is at the artists' full disposal to pay themselves a wage and develop their programmatic platforms.[102]

For a founder, the process of stepping away from an organization is complex. In making space for other voices, white people must be mindful not to dump the work on the shoulders of people of color without ensuring that capacities and support systems are in place. When a white cultural leader steps back from socially engaged work, it threatens to reify the assumption that socially engaged art is not white people's work, but the domain of people of color.

How can white people redistribute power without avoiding the structural work of anti-racism? In stepping back, how can white people not withdraw our resources, networks, and position, but connect people of color directly with these existing assets? When white leaders in the arts step back, it creates crucial opportunities for white donors to demonstrate more inclusive cultural philanthropy by investing in leaders of color, not only in historically white-led organizations undergoing leadership change, but also in organizations founded by and for people of color.[103]

Finally, distributing power in the arts can't happen in a vacuum. As organizational leadership changes, so too does its community and context. When a white-led arts organization evolves into one led or co-led by people of color, the organization must consider how these leadership changes impact its audience and community. The entire arts ecosystem must support these shifts. Funding patterns must prioritize organizations and initiatives led and founded by artists of color.[104] Funding opportunities should be open to organizations and projects working outside the realm of the traditional nonprofit. How can funders give artists direct access to funding opportunities without requiring them to partner with white-led organizations or organizations that don't share their values?

BARRIERS TO CHANGE

Given the benefits and potential of distributed leadership, why do outdated models in the dance field persist? Successful artistic and executive directors often prioritize the survival of their organizations above all else. Often arts organizations frame their logic of scarcity in terms of a business decision ("We're just trying to survive.") But inability or unwillingness to share power are not mere business decisions. These are emotionally charged habits of moving through the world. These habits can take the form of complacency, habit, self-interest, fear, ego, inertia, lack of imagination, and a sense of being underappreciated and even victimized. White people, "even those committed, in theory, to the struggle against white supremacy—do not know how to share power. White people do not know how to let white supremacy die without feeling like they themselves are dying."[105]

At the *Dancing Around Race* public gathering in 2019, Thomas DeFrantz put it this way:

> It's really hard for white people to get out of the way. It's training from before birth: "You own this. You get to decide." It's not about "letting other people [lead]" because then you're still there. But you figure out how to do your time and get out of the way. Open the space out and get out of the way. White domination/white supremacy replenishes itself…it will keep going. So you have to do more than get out of the way. You have to figure out the system that's in operation and figure out how to help disrupt it. You just got to do that work. There are other models of coalition leadership, leadership that's temporary but not inconsequential, leadership that's temporary but sustained through coalition-building that grows and expands through time. So that it's not, "This year, it's the Filipino year and this year, it's the Native year." It's not that, but a coalition of people that is able to expand from itself and shift whiteness out of the center and then again out of the margin while still controlling the center. But it's not easy. None of this is easy because these systems are super powerful. So we have to do the work of understanding how we're in them first and then we have to try to do the work of understanding how to take bits and pieces of them apart and reconstituting possibility among ourselves.[106]

Knowing when and how to "step back" can be confusing and difficult for many white artists and curators. Trans performance theorist Julian Carter asks, "What is the line between stepping back and retreating into white silence?"[107] When faced with challenges to their power, white people can assume a variety of defensive postures, including: denial, defensiveness, perfectionism, retreat into intellectualism, self-absorption, silence, criticism, numbness, and urgency.[108] These deeply ingrained defensive postures prevent white people from engaging fully in the work of confronting and changing existing power dynamics in the arts. In my own work transitioning HMD from a historically hierarchical arts organization into a model of distributed leadership, I have discovered that inside the gesture of stepping back, there is always a choice. I can step back and withdraw emotionally. Or I can step back and stay accountable and engaged. Choosing the latter requires that I resist ancient habits of avoiding emotional exposure. At times, a more accurate image for the work might be "stepping to the side": making space for other voices while staying in relationship.

Shifting cultural power gets hard when it gets personal. After years of struggling to build their careers, many white artists feel wronged if they forego opportunity. For white women, cultural equity and feminism can feel at odds: "stepping back" may feel contrary to feminist teachings that tell women to take up space. As a feminist and someone critical of women who renounce their voice in relationships, it's striking that I constantly find myself in professional situations where decentering myself is the right thing to do. These complexities can contribute to a failure of allyship even when intentions are good.[109] Again, how can I step back without disappearing? How can I show up in the world in a different way? I've spoken with several established white choreographers who support the sharing of power in some aspects of their organization, but draw the line at the studio door. "It's what I do," said one, explaining why she will not give up her role as a single-author choreographer. "It's who I am," echoed another. Sharing power challenges us to let go of the stories we tell about ourselves.

Not taking things personally is a prerequisite to sharing power. After the 2017 *Radical Movements* program, I received an anonymous letter criticizing me as a cis-white female for curating a program that explored the meaning of a radical body. The letter criticized the racial composition of the featured performers and speakers as overly white and called for greater trans and person of color (POC) leadership in programming. The letter demoralized me. Did they know how hard I had worked on that program? Did they know we lost money on that program? But I got over it. And redoubled my efforts to evolve our programming to center queer artists and artists of color. Faced with criticism, white people must check their reactions and make "a commitment not to panic, overread, or catastrophize."[110] This is "counterintuitive" for white people and takes work.[111]

Some questions that may prevent white curators, founders, and directors from relinquishing organizational power include: What about my career? Didn't I start the organization and build it from the ground up? Haven't I raised and managed all the money for all these years? The company has my name in it! Yes. And now it's time for change.

This work is larger than any one person or institution. Often, despite myself and despite my politics, I find myself perpetuating structures I want to disavow.[112] In the course of trying to hand over power, I catch myself focusing on my own interests; conversations about decentering whiteness often end up centering whiteness. These patterns are insidious even in the context of virtuous work. Prison abolitionist Ruth Wilson Gilmore says that "our focus should not be on organizational (or career) preservation, but on furthering the movement of which an organization is a part."[113] For white curators, curating as community organizing is about breaking habits of self-interest and logics of scarcity. In the studio, as artists we must ask, "What does the work need?" and "Who is the work for?" As curators and organizational leaders, the questions are the same. How can we respond with listening, observation, and imagination?

Shifting cultural power is a complex creative process that involves seeding new structures, dismantling old ones, and evolving others. DeFrantz describes this process at a *Dancing Around Race* public gathering in 2019:

> That's how institutions start to code-switch: they start to imagine not a singularity, but something more lateral. It will inevitably be more complicated. It won't be as simple as having one person everyone goes to and they answer everything. It'll be more like the challenge of creating, of allowing a community to emerge.[114]

We must bring the wisdom of our moving bodies to this work. Organizations tend to calcify. Contact improviser Steve Paxton says that "improvisation tends toward fixity."[115] In response, improvisers must not "strive to achieve results, but rather, to meet the constantly changing physical reality with appropriate placement and energy."[116] Like skilled dancers, we must constantly reawaken ourselves and our organizations to respond to a changing world. QTBIPOC Performing Artist Hive's mission statement reflects this idea: "This statement too will change as leadership circulates and evolves."[117] According to Cyndi Suarez, institutions "are simply the dead forms, or artifacts, that result from past power-laden interactions."[118] We can build authentic community by constantly aligning our intentions and our structures with collective liberation.

Chapter 3

Creating an Artist Commons

The emergence of new, transformative, even revolutionary
creativity... occurs at the juncture between the production of art and the
exercise of deep critical thought.
—*poet Garrett Hongo*[119]

A crucial part of shifting cultural power is building an artist commons—a safe space for multiple artist voices to be in meaningful exchange across difference. An artist commons protects the creative energy in a community, which can be damaged by a lack of a sense of continuity and historical validation.[120] An artist commons resists what writer Jenny Odell calls "context collapse," a condition facilitated by the ubiquity of social media, where artists lose touch with who their real community is.[121] An artist commons allows artists to find, as Adrienne Rich says, "whom we envision as our hearers, our co-creators, our challengers; who will urge us to take our work further, more seriously, than we had dared; on whose work we can build."[122] An artist commons provides a tangible, embodied context for making work: a support structure built on relationships, feedback, and exchange.

In their review of The Bridge Project's 2017 *Radical Movements* program, dance scholars Megan Nicely and Michelle Lavigne described the kinds of exchange present during that program as "an ongoing way of thinking-in-relation" that gives people the chance to relate "as a community rather than as separate entities," "to speak out loud while looking each other in the eye."[123] In prioritizing exchange, The Bridge Project takes what curator Maura Reilly calls "a relational approach" to curating, a strategy of curatorial resistance to the historic white male cultural dominance that creates space for a "polylogue," a term Reilly borrows from philosopher Julia Kristeva.[124]

Creating spaces for dialogue across difference is one of The Bridge Project's core curatorial strategies. Dialogue primes body and mind for questioning, which is an essential condition for both robust civic engagement and rigorous artmaking. The value of dialogue lies not in building agreement, but in providing an opportunity to get comfortable with discomfort. In this way, dialogue can be a powerful tool in destabilizing fixed identities and ideas.

Building an artist commons recognizes that:

- Critical thinking is a collective act.
- Critical thinking is a prerequisite for rigorous art practice.
- Critical thinking and artmaking are mutually supportive forms of deep listening.

Our most valuable critical thinking comes from an embodied, engaged relationship to the world. Isolation is a barrier to artistic growth. In the words of intersectional feminist scholar Sara Ahmed, "[i]t is the practical experience of coming up against a world that allows us to come up with new ideas, ideas that are not dependent on a mind that has withdrawn (because a world has enabled that withdrawal) but a body that has to wiggle about just to create room."[125] Below are case studies from The Bridge Project of building an artist commons through dialogue.

CASE STUDIES: GATHERING AROUND QUESTIONS
AESTHETIC EQUITY

In October 2019, The Bridge Project presented a workshop called *"Aesthetic equity is not _____ / aesthetic equity is_____ / visioning the reworking of everything, together,"* co-led by choreographers Liz Lerman and Paloma McGregor.[126] The workshop was cosponsored by Yayoi Kambara, one of the The Bridge Project's 2019–2020 Community Engagement Residency lead artists, in conjunction with Kambara's project, *Aesthetic Shift: A Dance Lab for Equitable Practices.* Kambara and I decided that it would be better to have this workshop co-led by Lerman and an artist of color, so we approached Lerman to select a co-facilitator. Lerman selected McGregor, with whom she had collaborated previously.

The *Aesthetic Equity* workshop was only four hours long, but it was a generative and powerful experience of creating an artist commons through gathering around questions. Crucially, the workshop did not happen in a vacuum, but in the wake of a year-long series of public events around race in dance as part of Gerald Casel's *Dancing Around Race* (discussed in depth in Chapter 4). Kambara was a member of Casel's artist cohort. As a result of this momentum, the *Aesthetic Equity* workshop attracted a group of about fifty people from many different dance communities within the Bay Area. There were older white artists, young artists of color, administrators, funders, writers, and artists from disciplines other than dance.

Rather than attempt to involve the entire room in one conversation, Lerman and McGregor expertly facilitated a space wherein a multitude of small conversations happened simultaneously. In small groups, participants discussed what they thought aesthetic equity was and what it was not. After these discussions, Lerman and McGregor invited each small group to move in the space in a way that reflected their experience of the discussion. In this way, participants translated their critical thinking into embodied experience. For example, if someone had felt alienated or excluded from a conversation, they stood far away from the people in their small group. In this way, physical embodiment reflected content that may have gone unspoken. Lerman and McGregor prompted another series of small group conversations with open-ended phrases related to creative practice such as, "I like to warm-up by…"; "When I negotiate a contract, I…"; "When I want to be creative, I…"; "When I collaborate, I…"; and "I find the people I want to work with by…." Participants self-selected which of these prompts to gather around with others. Other exercises invited pairs to take a walk outside as they held a conversation.

The workshop was heavy on dialogue, with less emphasis on movement. But for many involved, the workshop generated thinking that supported their movement practice. One participant reflected:

> [The workshop] inspired me to have conversations with artists about our creative process. It supported me to connect with two other artists I've wanted to connect with for a while. We are starting a new body of work together out of that conversation![127]

But many artists of color who participated left the workshop feeling exhausted from doing white people's emotional work. In the words of one participant:

> The workshop reminded me of why I don't attend equity workshops anymore as a POC. I will continue to work with my people and allies who are conscious of race and don't avoid it. I'm tired of doing the work for white people. They need to do their own work. Once they do that, we can all come together for collective action.[128]

The difference in feedback from the above participants surfaces a crucial question for curators: Who is the work for? When is it productive to convene an event for the general public? When is it more productive to create space that is only for people of color or only for white people? When do we move separately? When do we come together?

It's tempting to say a training, discussion, or workshop about cultural equity is for everyone. But people are at different places in their learning. When you put white people who have not given serious thought to cultural and racial equity in the same room with artists of color who have thought about the issue for their entire lives, finding a common language is frustrating for everyone. Choreographer and curator Bhumi B. Patel, former HMD Program Coordinator and now on HMD's Board of Directors, states:

> The big issue that I often see in arts equity work is that the programming sets up the expectation that everyone is coming from the same place. This is not true. Folks who have lived experiences of racism and marginalization do not need the 101. One of the more successful ways I've seen this mitigated is through affinity groupings during trainings. POCs have different needs in these moments and white folks need to have the space to be with other white folks to communicate their thoughts and feelings. I want to continue to interrogate the models for gathering to center marginalized voices in the space.[129]

Again and again I hear from artists of color that they are sick of attending events where they are asked to do white people's work for them. When we convene public events around race and frame the event as being for everyone, we set up artists of color to carry the burden of educating white people. As white people, we need to assume responsibility for educating ourselves. How can we acknowledge that we come from different positions in relationship to cultural equity? Format shapes outcomes. Public-facing, community-wide conversations may not always be the most generative format. This is not to say that we must stay siloed off from each other. But as curators, it's our job to be mindful about how we come together. How can we create safe space while also ensuring that we work through conflict?

During the writing of this book, HMD staff, Liz Lerman, Paloma McGregor, and Yayoi Kambara planned a follow-up workshop to *Aesthetic Equity*. In our planning, we discussed how to name, acknowledge, and financially compensate POC labor in the multiracial setting of the workshop. As one response, we decided to offer stipends to a group of artists of color from Kambara's Community Engagement Residency cohort to co-facilitate along with Lerman and McGregor. In this way, we explicitly acknowledged the emotional labor involved for artists of color participating in a workshop about race with white people. In order to address the fact that white people and POCs come to cultural equity work from different places, Kambara suggested that we pair the *Aesthetic Equity 2* workshop with an anti-racism training that would be required for any white folks interested in attending *Aesthetic Equity 2,* but not required for POCs. We also discussed having white people and POCs work in separate affinity groups and making it clear to white people that they would be showing up for a POC-centered space, not a space intended to accommodate them.

REORGANIZING OURSELVES

Another model for creating an artist commons by gathering around questions occurred in The Bridge Project's 2015 program *Rewriting Dance*, which featured *Reorganizing Ourselves*, a collaborative project among curator Michèle Steinwald, choreographer Deborah Hay, and philosopher Alva Noë. This event featured solo performative lectures by Noë and Hay followed by a community circle of questions facilitated by Steinwald. The project's culminating community circle phase was the driving force in creating an experience of the artist commons for those who attended. The community circle was neither a Q&A format nor an audience discussion. Instead, Steinwald asked everyone in the circle to pose a question about the work they had just experienced. This was how Steinwald opened the circle:

Michèle Steinwald: We've all been a part of the same experiment, but we all have our own unique experiences with it. Because we'll all be in dialogue, I'd like to start by asking everyone's name.

[*Everyone in the room says their name*]

Michèle Steinwald: I'd like us to start in asking questions. Really thinking about the material we've just experienced. That's our experiment. What was your experience? Ask a question. Anybody can start.

Deborah Hay: Michèle, you mean we are all asking questions.

Michèle Steinwald: Yeah. I think everybody should ask a question based on the material.¹³⁰

As it became clear that these questions were not meant to be answered, the room settled into asking questions as a practice. It was comforting to be in a room full of questions where a state of not knowing and not understanding was normal and encouraged. Being with other people in a state of unknowing was a form of intimacy. In the space of a short time, the format of the event created a sense of an artist commons and legitimized an approach to artmaking rooted in critical thinking.

RADICAL MOVEMENTS: GENDER AND POLITICS IN PERFORMANCE

The Bridge Project's 2017 program, *Radical Movements: Gender and Politics in Performance*, was an entire festival rooted in a question. It gathered fifteen artists and thinkers, most of whom identified as queer and/or POC, in dialogue and performance in response to the prompt, "What does it mean to have a radical body?"

The festival created multiple spaces for audience members to examine gender through hybrid performance structures and alternative formats for audience engagement. The program included The Bridge Project's first Audience Reader, a compilation of readings designed to encourage critical thinking around the festival's themes; six performance events, many of which incorporated dialogue between artists on stage and between artists and audience members; discussion following every performance; a mid-week Audience Salon to discuss the performances and the Reader; and a culminating community gathering. The festival created space for exchanges "between bodies and words," and "gestured to possible models for how radical social movement might be formed and recognized":¹³¹

> [*Radical Movements*] sought to generate dialogue within the Bay Area performance community by posing various dialogic exchanges as performance. Events subverted common formats such as the often unsatisfying post-show talk-back or scholarly lecture that maintains a certain hierarchy in relation to an artist where audiences consume, moderators and scholars explain, and performers labor. Importantly, during these numerous events, conversations arose in real time, giving the sense that "radical performance" is not about planning which boundaries might be transgressed but rather, in the words of artist Monique Jenkinson, about "accepting complexity."¹³²

Ordinary Practices of the Radical Body, part of the *Radical Movements* program, was a commissioned performance lecture by gender theorist Judith Butler and performance-maker/drag queen Monique ("Fauxnique") Jenkinson. Butler and Jenkinson entered the stage together "as if they just happened to meet up on a dance floor at some hip theory club, tapping their feet and swaying their hips to the beat of the dance music:"[133]

> They did not talk right away, allowing us to take in the scene—they were warming up their bodies before they started their verbal exchange. They danced around the stage casually in this way for some time, discussing their bodily practices, early dance experiences, and gender theories. Their conversation seemed planned but not fully scripted, allowing their speech to flow with ease yet stay on track.[134]

Dance critic Sima Belmar called *Ordinary Practices of the Radical Body* "the greatest lec-dem of all time," saying that Butler and Jenkinson's dancing "demonstrated that the philosopher has a body and the dancer has a mind—in other words, everyone is a bodymind—and the toll dancing and scholarly labor takes on the body was made visible by their talk about it."[135]

Following is an excerpt from the transcript of the hour-long performance of *Ordinary Practices of the Radical Body*. Jenkinson begins the piece by addressing the audience directly:

Monique Jenkinson: We're both here because of drag.

Judith Butler: Yes. Can you talk to us a little bit about the work you do and how you got into being Fauxnique and Ms. Trannyshack 2003?

MJ: That was 13 years ago. I came to San Francisco as a little dancer. Going back before that, I was a little ballerina. I knew I needed something that wasn't ballet, but I didn't really know what it was. So I went to the farthest thing from that I could find, which was Bennington College, a place where you show up and they're like, "Here's the studio. Go make work." I showed up in my little shiny blue unitard and my bun. The Bennington College version of a mean girl was contemporary-dance-serious-girl who was like, "Why do you shave your armpits?" Bennington and the San Francisco dance scene at the time were very steeped in the Judson aesthetic: the aesthetic of Yvonne Rainer, the "no manifesto," an aesthetic of refusal where we were all dancing in our sweats, not acknowledging the audience, and having an internal experience. At the same time I was reading theory. I was trying to read Judith Butler.

JB: I'm sorry. Forgive me.

MJ: No, it was great. But I realized what I needed was some glitter, some sequins.

JB: You were looking for glamour.

MJ: A friend of mine dragged me to the drag clubs. I fell in love with Tranny-shack. The club name has since changed.

JB: We honor the history.

MJ: That was when I fell in love with the drag show. I became a screaming fan. Through drag, I rediscovered ballet.

JB: How did you become a theory queen?

MJ: Hashtag I could die happy. Judith Butler just called me a theory queen. It was by practice. What was your experience in the club? Where did you come to it?

JB: I went to school in New Haven. There was a bar called Partners. Downstairs were mainly lesbians who were doing line dancing or debating separatism or breaking up. They did a lot of breaking up down there. That was cool for a while but I would always drift upstairs, gay men, drinking, dancing. Magnificent drag shows in '77, '78, again '81, '82. As I think about drag, I have to think about what was my spectatorial passion in relation to drag. It was like, this is fabulous. This is gorgeous. This is perfect. This is incredible. When you saw that freedom of expression in the most radical way at least for me at that time, it seemed very amazing. They were doing girlness and femininity in a way with freedom and love and passion in a way that I could never do. I never wanted to do. Everybody told me I should do. I can't do. I was so far away from that, but I loved it. Right? It wasn't me, but it was what I loved.

MJ: Did you have to kind of reconcile drag with feminism? In that moment, were you identifying as a feminist lesbian?

JB: No. I was a feminist. I am a feminist. I was a lesbian. I'm still arguably something. I'm legally nonbinary now. But the truth is that I was crossing over then easily and happily. There were massively transphobic forms of feminism that were already there or sometimes quite explicit. That's not to say that drag's the same as trans. I know it's not, though they're linked. Some feminists thought that drag was an over-appropriation of femininity, but who owns femininity?

Have we ever yet seen somebody who has that as property? I don't think so. It's not property.

MJ: This comes back to who is allowed to do drag. When I started doing drag some people said, you're appropriating drag from gay men. I thought, "You're imitating *me*, queen!" What is authenticity in the performance? I realized that drag was a vernacular and a voice I needed to be working in and that I had already been doing drag. The moment I put on false eyelashes for the Nutcracker, I knew this is what my face is supposed to look like. I needed that artifice.

JB: Yes.

MJ: The artifice was the authenticity. It wasn't like, "Oh, we are now neutral, we are now authentic." The practice of ballet is also drag. Ballet as a practice is a super codified way of being feminine. So when you were at Bennington, is that when you met Wendy Perron?

JB: Yeah, we were pals.

MJ: She was the editor of *Dance Magazine*.

JB: We would hang out in New York. As you know, summers in New York can be unbearable. We were walking around. There were these very fancy restaurants. Nobody was making any money, we were students. A group of us started doing some funny movements on the street, especially in front of the very fancy restaurants. There would be people who would peep behind the window.

MJ: So this is the window to the restaurants [*gestures to the wall of the theater*].

JB: This is the window. We decided that we would collapse in front of the windows.

MJ: Did you actually touch the window?

JB: Sometimes, yes. We would begin to lose our balance. Then we would kind of dive [*dives against the wall and begins to fall to the floor*].

MJ: Oh my god, that's amazing.

JB: We would wait to see whether the good bourgeois people were alarmed that somebody had collapsed outside the window.

MJ: Were they?

JB: I think they were a little horrified, in the way the bourgeois horror works. They didn't run out and say, "Oh my god." [*the two continue to fall against the wall*]

MJ: The collapse.

JB: Full collapse.

MJ: You see a lot of choreographies of collapse going on right now.

JB: It poses the question of who might catch you. Where you might land. Whether there is a ground or a floor for you in this life. Or whether they've all been taken away or defunded. Whether you've got insurance. Whether people you live near will stop and help you.

MJ: You've said no one stands alone.

JB: Even now, if I don't have shoes, I'm not able to dance because I have joint problems. It does seem to me that we depend on all kinds of floors and grounds. The question is whether we find a ground that can hold us when we fall.[136]

Ordinary Practices of the Radical Body was one event among many in the *Radical Movements* festival that created space for dialogue and critical thinking in the context of performance itself. In their review of *Radical Movements*, Maxe Crandall and Selby Schwartz wrote:

> The Bridge Project reimagines and even celebrates conversation as a form that brings us body to body. What can we do, together, with the bodies that we have? And what can we do with the bodies that we have together? At the conjured intersections between different ways of doing, these collaborations suggest how we can tend to the queer bonds between bodies and ideas. Radical movements, both physical and political, sometimes remain in the realm of the airy, the ideational, the abstract; they only become movements when you do what you say. In both cases, there is risk; in both cases, there is togetherness.[137]

CASE STUDY: SUPPORTING REFUSAL
THE COMMUNITY ENGAGEMENT RESIDENCY

The Bridge Project's Community Engagement Residency, which started in 2017, came at a time when many dance organizations across the US began prioritizing support for artists of color and projects geared toward racial equity, including the Dance/USA Fellowships to Artists, Race Forward's Racial

Equity in the Arts Innovation Lab, Gibney's Moving Toward Justice in New York City, Aesthetic Perspectives in Pittsburgh, and The Equity Project: Increasing the Presence of Blacks in Ballet, a project of Dance Theatre of Harlem, The International Association of Blacks in Dance, and Dance/USA, among others.[138] The Bridge Project's Community Engagement Residency supports artists for a full year to engage in community, however they define it. The program supports artists to build artist commons on their own terms. As of this writing, of twelve CER lead artists, ten have been artists of color.

Performance artist Julie Tolentino was the first lead artist in The Bridge Project's Community Engagement Residency. Her year-long residency combined group studio practice, solo practice, and performance. Tolentino navigated among these three modes throughout the year, allowing each to inform the other. Questions that she held throughout her residency included, in her words:

– What is and who offers sanctuary?
– What do I dare need?
– How do we work within the wide abstract of words, worlds and of the ongoing stratification of race, sex, gender, and class?
– Am I able to facilitate a space of the unknown—that includes the vulnerability of being part of the group?
– How can I produce artist and audience agency through such methods as optimistic refusal, aesthetic geometry, awkward affect, and time-based discovery?
– What matters to (each of) us?
– What is my role with or for each artist? Do these interactions constitute community-building?[139]

Tolentino began by developing studio practices with a cohort of four artists she named "The Hard Corps": Maurya Kerr, Amara Tabor-Smith, Xandra Ibarra, and Larry Arrington. After nine months of shared and one-on-one studio practice, Tolentino and the group presented *a.u.l.e. (an un-named lived experience)*, a practice in performance that also featured Tolentino's long-time colleagues Debra Levine and Scot Nakagawa as writers embedded in the installation. This event took place as part of The Bridge Project's 2017 *Radical Movements* program.

a.u.l.e. took place in low light over a period of three hours. The performers practiced an interlocking set of movement scores developed both individually and in groups through the preceding months of studio work with Tolentino.

The performers arranged and operated rolling lights on dimmers and experimented with improvising with each other using body, sound, text, movement, and materials that included, in the words of Debra Levine, dozens of inanimate objects "not directed toward capital consumption:" (p)leather, thread, dead plants, herbs, scents, a light box with hundreds of slides of the artists taken from their studio work and sound by Patrick Murch and Tolentino.[140] The audience was free to move, stand, or sit anywhere in the space. Tolentino facilitated the entire experience and intervened in the installation by reading text, layering sound, and composing the space. She was both inside and outside of the work, participating from the margins and listening to the work from the inside. The group's blurring of the line between practice and performance was "an invitation" toward new forms of community.[141]

Embedded writers Nakagawa and Levine wrote in response to the action and in conversation with each other. Their texts, scrolling in real time on two adjacent walls, situated the performance in San Francisco's history and were "both an asynchronous conversation and solo musings based in memory, associations, theoretical and political perspectives, and shared embodied experiences such as living through the AIDS crisis and participating in ACT UP and other kinds of activism."[142]

Following *a.u.l.e.*, Tolentino decided that she needed to shift away from group work and focus on her solo studio process. A solo working period of three months culminated in *.bury.me.fiercely,*[143] which integrated the group work of The Hard Corps with Tolentino's longstanding solo performance practices and implemented several of Tolentino's signature methods: in her words, "durational performance, movement, exploration of abstraction and minimalism with aims to seduce the project into its barest presentational form."[144] *.bury. me.fiercely.* featured video using the names of the artists from The Hard Corps and light box images that lit slides of the individual artists and ephemeral material from the group's process, including artist writings and scents created from the group's collaboration with herbalist Jennie Patterson. The work offered, in Tolentino's words, the body as "a landscape, a container of record, and a living archive through the lens of raced, illegible, and tethered lives."[145]

Although Tolentino's year-long residency had elements of practice familiar to many artists, the context felt different. At the outset of the residency, Tolentino and I agreed that the scope and nature of the work could shift throughout the year. Working together, we moved slowly, exchanging constant feedback, providing mutual support, and allowing the work to unfold and change course on its own terms. This kind of work and witness requires time, flexibility, and responsiveness on both sides. It required us to move at the speed of relationship, not production.

I am grateful to Tolentino for showing me the importance, in creating safe spaces for artists, of supporting artist refusal. I use the word *refusal* to refer to many different kinds of aesthetic and political refusal, including refusals of clarity, visibility, legibility, and accessibility.[146] Socially engaged art has long been framed as a form of "encounter."[147] Refusal is its own form of encounter, with its own legitimate aesthetics and politics. According to Herbert Marcuse, "refusal must not only be the guiding principle for all artistic creation, it must also be a manifestation of artistic creation itself."[148] Art critic Claire Bishop talks about refusal in terms of "antagonism," a term she uses to refer to "a criticality and a resistance to intelligibility" that she calls "necessary for aesthetics."[149] Critical indigenous studies scholars have theorized that recognition and visibility can perpetuate colonial regimes of knowledge and power.[150] Likewise, Jack Halberstam's *Queer Art of Failure* frames failure as "a way of refusing to acquiesce to dominant logics of power and discipline and […] a form of critique."[151]

Many choreographers and dance forms work with slowness as a form of refusal (Maria Hassabi, Okwui Okpokwasili, Hana Erdman, Bodycartography Project, and Butoh artists, to name but a few). But rarely does slowness enter the curator-artist relationship as a value in itself. White artists have long had the luxury of refusal.[152] Part of shifting cultural power is granting the power of refusal to all artists on and off stage.

REFUSING PRESSURES FOR CLARITY AND URGENCY

Working with Tolentino and other artists through The Bridge Project's Community Engagement Residency has shown me that refusing pressures for clarity and urgency is a necessary part of supporting artists working in community. Socially engaged art is "above all, process-oriented. It has to take into consideration not only the formal mechanisms within art itself, but also how it will reach its context and audience and why."[153] Socially engaged art projects "might mean a connection with some community or group of people for years, maybe some artist's whole life. It's hard to bring to the public. Sometimes it's hard to define."[154] Deena Chalabi, formerly the head of Public Knowledge at SFMOMA, writes that processes in which artists are encouraged to take their time to develop their ideas in community tend "to require a different level of comfort with publicly sharing process rather than simply a final product."[155]

One feature of white supremacy culture[156] is a sense of urgency, which can make it difficult to take time for thoughtful decision-making and long-term visioning.[157] Bhumi B. Patel says: "Institutions want things done on schedules and processing emotional labor and dismantling racism cannot be done on a schedule. I want this work to have the contingency to breathe and take breaks and have space."[158] It can be challenging to translate artist-led community process into conversations with funders, who often want quantitative metrics of success, or into marketing campaigns, which demand the promotion of a product. Another feature of white supremacy culture is worship of the written word: if it's not written down, it doesn't exist. And yet success in this work is often personal, qualitative, and mysterious. Often, its implications only become clear years later.

As a field rooted in expression beyond language, dance is uniquely positioned to appreciate the power of ambiguity. In *dance of darkness: a performance, a conversation, a rehearsal for the future*—a performance lecture by Jack Halberstam and boychild, also known as Tosh, commissioned for The Bridge Project's 2017 *Radical Movements* program—Halberstam and boychild refused to impose clarity on boychild's dancing body:

JH: There's an expectation that the artist somehow knows what they're doing. I'm not saying that Tosh doesn't know what he's doing. But it's nice to talk through what his performance grammar is and to not feel like we always have to just go with the artist's truth, because we're all making sense of what we see. I was trying to push towards not making sense of it and allowing it to stand in its complexity. We don't tether it to clear ideas that illuminate it. That's good information for me about how to approach a performance text. It's a risk to come into a space like this. You don't know if it will work or not.

boychild: Yeah, got to be ready for a complete failure. The good stuff comes out of failure.

JH: Failure might be a nice place to end.[159]

Cultural strategy activist Nayantara Sen writes, "[w]hen it comes to cultural transformation, clarity is not always the best goal."[160] Curators committed to shifting cultural power "must be comfortable navigating conditions that are murky, unclear, diffuse, and highly complex."[161] Instead of seeking clarity, people interested in supporting and making art that shifts cultural power will, as Sen says, "benefit from pursuing a diversity of tactics that support experimentation, testing, replication, reframing, and scaling of their ideas."[162] Shifting cultural power demands a re-visioning of the terms of creative engagement and the meaning of success—a re-visioning that refuses the traps of urgency and clarity.

REFUSING PRESSURES FOR VISIBILITY

The long-term work of creating an artist commons also requires honoring artist needs to refuse visibility. In *dance of darkness*, Jack Halberstam talked about the politics of visibility:

> When we say, "We want visibility," we tend to be actually feeding into a polit-
> ical cycle that we would be better off out of.... Some people are made for
> visibility and many people are not. Early pride parades didn't want drag
> queens at the forefront. The latest political movements around gay marriage
> are also about coming into visibility for the state in the way that the state
> wants you to, as opposed to resisting inscription and insisting upon other
> forms of being.[163]

Creating a commons for artists means allowing artists to define the terms of their visibility. Refusal of visibility can have both aesthetic and practical dimensions. The aesthetics of refusal are present in many aspects of Julie Tolentino's work, such as bodies obscured by fabric or wigs and installations in conditions of low light.[164] Questions around how to translate refusal of dominant culture into aesthetics have been a main concern of Yayoi Kambara's 2019 Community Engagement Residency, *Aesthetic Shift: A Lab for Equitable Practices*, which asks: "How do we unlearn externally imposed aesthetics (learned dance lineages) ingrained in our body in order to access authentic physical vocabulary and creative practice that aligns with equity values?"[165]

All artists need inward-looking space. In particular, artists who make work that challenges the dominant culture need space that refuses its gaze. Writer Reni Eddo-Lodge talks about why it is important for women of color to meet without white feminists: "That gaze does so much to silence you.... Even if you're really confident and really vocal, there is still a holding back that you have to do."[166] Refusal of visibility can take the form of refusing to have an event be open to the public or to white people. Latinx choreographer David Herrera, a 2019 Community Engagement Residency lead artist, reflected that because he trained inside a white dance lineage, he could not find a sense of community in the dance world. Herrera said that for many years, "I kept my identity at bay." It was only when he "stopped catering to white aesthetics" that he no longer felt a separation between his identity and dance.[167] Part of shifting cultural power is creating spaces where artists of color can bring their full selves to the room. Creating that space often involves some form of refusal.

Both artmaking and activism require strategic alternation between openness and closure.[168] Martin Luther King, Jr., in planning the Montgomery bus boycott, used meetings of all sizes and in a wide range of contexts, from people's homes to large public meetings. It was at the smaller, internal meetings that King and his colleagues "strategized how to run the larger meetings, collaborating quickly and intensely on ideas that would be put into play in successively wider contexts."[169] Paul Chan's *Waiting for Godot in New Orleans* (2007) applied many tools of community organizing to realize the work of live performance: behind the production was eight months of workshops, teaching, potluck dinners, and fundraising for post-Katrina rebuilding efforts. But these political activities made possible the artmaking process itself—the actual rehearsal process—a place where, according to Chan, things like politics didn't matter anymore.[170]

Gathering and working in private spaces is a crucial part of public engagement. Gerald Casel's 2018 Community Engagement Residency featured monthly gatherings behind closed doors; this series of inward-looking meetings paralleled a series of public events. The private gatherings were a kind of sanctuary for the artists and a space to strategize about how to approach the public events. One of the 2019 Community Engagement Residencies, the QTBIPOC Performing Artist Hive, regularly holds events that are only open to people who identify as QTBIPOC. When we first started the 2019 residency program, we required all lead artists to hold at least two "public-facing" events during the year. At some point, we faced this question: If an event was open only to artists of color, could that count as "public-facing"? We decided that it could.

Dominant culture equates visibility with success (How many followers do you have on social media? How much press coverage did your event garner?) Foundations ask us to measure our impact in terms of audience members. Activist culture can uphold these same assumptions (How did you get the message out? How many people came to the protest?).

We must be careful to avoid replicating the same structures that we want to challenge. How can we measure impact in terms of relationships, not numbers? After four years of our Community Engagement Residency, we have adjusted expectations around public-facing events. As we honor artist's need to turn inward, our audience numbers drop. Following the lead of the cultural strategy sector, evaluation in the arts must "capture and understand shifts in quantity and quality of relationships and networks over time":

> To assess cultural impact, the most appropriate longitudinal evaluation strategies are those that measure long-term future-facing, visionary, and proactive framing, stories, and ideas. There are many measurement tools that are good for retrospective analysis and short- to medium-term impact assessment and planning. To understand cultural shifts, though, you need indicators that point to changes in the cultural pulse of your community. Those indicators should identify proactive, visionary frames—rather than reactive responses. In your work, look for data points that demonstrate how shifts in language and behaviors are being picked up, disseminated, internalized, and validated across echo chambers and encapsulated spaces such as regions or states.[171]

Approaching culture as a way of building community asks us to look at the arts through a movement-building lens—in terms of relationships—not just through a production lens, which tends evaluate success in terms of tickets sold, audience members served, and other deliverables. Reporting pressures from funders can lead nonprofit arts organizations to frame everything in terms of success and, in a desire to achieve preconceived results, to repeat the same strategies. Being responsive to community requires flexibility. It calls on us to slow down, listen, and imagine new ways of defining success.

Chapter 4

Inviting Difficult Conversations

CASE STUDY

DANCING AROUND RACE

Part of shifting cultural power is inviting difficult conversations. An artist commons should be a safe space, but not necessarily a harmonious one. It can be chaotic and fractured. Culture itself is messy. One aspect of white supremacy culture is the "right to comfort (the belief that those with power have a right to emotional and psychological comfort)," so discomfort, especially on the part of white people, is often a prerequisite for cultural change.[172] Curators need to frame discomfort as an essential and generative space for inquiry, rather than as something to be avoided.[173] Rather than strive to create tidy, feel-good spaces of agreement, we "must not stop and enjoy a cathartic release until we have achieved justice."[174] In the words of Ibram X. Kendi, "[w]hen it comes to healing America of racism, we want to heal America without pain, but without pain, there is no progress."[175]

In the second year of the Community Engagement Residency (2018–2019), lead artist Gerald Casel developed and led a project called *Dancing Around Race*. Like Tolentino, Casel chose a small cohort of artists to work with for the year: Raissa Simpson, Zulfikar Ali Bhutto, Sammay Dizon, Yayoi Kambara and David Herrera. Casel described *Dancing Around Race*:

For this residency, I will be engaging with artists as co-interrogators to look closely at the role race plays in dance production and presentation. We will ask how our work as artists functions in society and how the communities we engage with are considered, internalized, and reflected through our work. Employing a "systems thinking" approach, I hope to connect with sectors of the Bay Area dance ecology and beyond to engage in invigorated dialogue to better understand how all are interconnected. We will invite curators, critics, scholars, dance writers, grantors, collaborators, publicists, and audience members to come together to spark conversations around dance. We will address systems of support, power and privilege, race and colorblind racial ideology, issues and problems around diversity, resilience, and sustainability, and more. Working with the premise that all sectors are interdependent, we will promote a culture of empathy so that every part of the dance community feels more visible, heard, and understood. Finally, we will identify issues that dancers, choreographers, and their collaborators face and will try to create solutions to problems that may be attributed to misunderstandings, uninformed assumptions, and myths.[176]

How do we create safe containers for difficult exchange? Throughout *Dancing Around Race*, we wrestled with whether the project needed a professional facilitator. We hired a professional facilitator for the first public gathering. Then, feeling like the facilitator was occupying space intended to be filled by lead artist Casel, we proceeded without them. Casel has a nonhierarchical leadership style that leaves plenty of space in the room for people to come forward and participate. I felt that my role was to step back and make space for other voices in the room. The combination of a lack of a professional facilitator, Casel's hands-off leadership style, and my desire to decenter myself left a wide open space for a stew of voices to surface.

Many different axes of power and privilege were at play in the project's public conversations. The conversations surfaced sadness, rage, and friction. Some people appreciated the opportunity to, as The Bridge Project's Co-Director Karla Quintero states, "acknowledge, listen, see, hear, to sit in different permutations of community, let the desire to exchange emerge, and let hardened fear, distrust, and disinterest in difference disintegrate."[177] But many others emerged from *Dancing Around Race*'s events dissatisfied and with a sense of the vast distances within the dance community. Some people were so upset by the events that they vowed never to attend such gatherings again. The *Dancing Around Race* events exposed how nascent dialogue around race is in the ostensibly liberal Bay Area and illuminated the need for more public discussion around race in the arts.[178]

At the project's culminating public event, there were over one hundred people packed into a small room. The event began with a presentation by Casel and guest speaker, scholar, and artist Thomas DeFrantz, followed by fifteen minutes of small group discussion, followed by a version of a "Long Table" discussion, a discussion format created by Lois Weaver.[179] Bhumi B. Patel, *Dancing Around Race*'s Program Coordinator, described the final public gathering this way:

> The room sizzled with an appropriately uncomfortable air—the majority of folks in attendance were white, and for most white folks, the discussion about race creates a deep anxiety and uncertainty. I felt a kind of stubborn rage that wouldn't settle. To me, it is an indirect ask for the oppressed and marginalized to create comfort for those in power through their uncompensated labor. That isn't the labor I showed up to do.[180]

Some people bemoaned the lack of more in-depth, sustained conversation at the *Dancing Around Race* events. In part, this indicated how dialogue around race in the Bay Area dance world remains in its infancy. Some attributed the lack of deeper dialogue at the events to format: for example, there needed to be more time for small group discussion. Others, like Karla Quintero, attributed the lack of productive exchange to the personal, charged nature of the sharing: "sometimes sharing the personal prevents conversation from happening and separates rather than brings together."[181] An additional barrier to deeper dialogue was a lack of clarity about who the events were for.

One advantage of being an independent curator is that you can implement programs without being slowed down by institutional bureaucracy. But *Dancing Around Race* showed me that implementing programs quickly has its risks. Some people questioned the wisdom behind inviting the public to a large, unfacilitated gathering on a highly charged subject. An HMD Advisory Board member, speaking confidentially, asked me, "Would an inexperienced choreographer invite the public to a big unfinished show?" But the work of shifting cultural power isn't a show; it's a process. And sometimes you have to dive into the mess. Because historical racial hierarchies tell white people that they are entitled to peace and deference, there is value in troubling and illuminating what Robin DiAngelo calls "white fragility." Discomfort can be a measure of a program's success.

Another measure of success of *Dancing Around Race* was the strength of the relationships it fostered among the artists involved. *Dancing Around Race* built lasting relationships: all of the artists in Casel's cohort remain close and continue to collaborate on artistic projects. *Dancing Around Race* continues long after the residency's end. *Dancing Around Race* Program Coordinator Patel reflected:

> I learned quite a lot from my involvement in *Dancing Around Race*. I learned how other POC artists are working through similar experiences to mine; I learned more about the fear and hesitation that white communities have about relinquishing power to POCs; I learned that the successful POCs have either found a corner to work in OR have code-switched themselves into being palatable to white people. I learned that I want a different future than the one that has been sold to me about my future in the arts. I learned that I have faith that we can create a better future, that we can, through this work, make a difference. I wasn't sure that I had that hope and faith prior to having the opportunity to be in community with DAR.[182]

For the artists directly involved in the cohort, *Dancing Around Race* made space to dig into important questions, including "how dance training leaves legacies of white dominance in the body; how our standards of excellence continue to be shaped by white aesthetic traditions; and how work made in those traditions (specifically ballet) receives disproportionate funding and attention."[183] Gerald Casel reflected on *Dancing Around Race* at its conclusion:

> I can honestly say that the residency changed my thinking and way of being in this dance community. Having taken a systems thinking approach has also allowed me to see—with greater clarity—how each of us and each institution are all interdependent. I also understand how badly this work is needed in this community. I hope to continue creating spaces like these for difficult conversations to be had so that we move forward with respect for each other and so that we can remove the invisible forces that detract from our potential as artists.[184]

Several times, people suggested to me that HMD was profiting financially off *Dancing Around Race*. HMD has not made money off these programs. Almost all of the funding we have received has gone directly to the lead artists, their artist cohorts, subsidizing space, and paying guest artist fees. Some years, grants don't cover the full expense of the Community Engagement Residency, so we must use operational funds to cover the difference; other years, grants have covered about five percent of staff pay. We are learning to be increasingly transparent with artists about project budgets, how much of a grant covers the project, and how much of a grant HMD is taking for non-project or general operating expenses like staff time.

Criticism of HMD regarding our financial self-interest with regard to projects like *Dancing Around Race* led me again to reckon with my intentions and my privilege. Mistrust from artists of color forces me to reckon with the realities of alliance. If I assume that artists of color work with me because they trust me, I ignore the history of racism. Perhaps we must begin by acknowledging strategic alignments—that artists of color are not working with white-led institutions out of trust, but because they understandably would like some funding and the opportunity to benefit from the organization's position in the field. Also, in San Francisco, as of this writing, almost every single dance presenting venue is run by a white person. So artists of color have no choice but to work with a white-led institution if they want to put their work into the world. In this context, white curators must build trust, not take it for granted.

Artist mistrust of my motivations behind supporting *Dancing Around Race* summoned what scholar George Lipsitz has called the "white spatial imaginary," where white intervention presents itself as an ethical act, rather than as a facet of Black and Brown oppression.[185] Robin DiAngelo points out that white progressives with good intentions do the most daily damage to people of color.[186] How is my involvement in anti-racist work self-serving? How can my commitment go deeper than optics? What does it mean to decenter myself not just in a room, but financially? As the funding landscape shifts in favor of supporting cultural equity, white institutions are trying to reposition themselves as allies. How does allyship preserve and perpetuate white self-interest? Is it enough for me, as a white curator, to decenter myself in the dance world? Would it be best if I left the field altogether?

At the end of the last *Dancing Around Race* public gathering as part of Casel's residency, full of uncomfortable emotions, I went up to my colleague Bhumi B. Patel. "Should I stop doing this work? Should HMD cease to exist?" I asked her. She paused, smiled, and answered: "It's complicated." In retrospect, I wish I had not leaked my distress and discomfort into Bhumi's lap; this is typical white behavior when faced with challenges to their power. I'm grateful that Bhumi and I have stayed in relationship; she now sits on HMD's Board of Directors. A year later, in writing this book, I asked her, "When do you think white-led arts organizations should be dismantled entirely?" She responded, "I think white-led arts organizations should be dismantled yesterday."[187]

Chapter 5

Facilitating Hybrid Forms

The performance equivalent of inviting difficult conversations—spaces where people must leave their comfort zone to meet each other—is hybrid form. Hybrid forms of performance, like the performative lecture, cross discipline and combine modes of address. By opening up liminal space between classification systems, they challenge societal structures. Hybrid forms have the potential to build bridges across difference by allowing performers, thinkers, and activists to "step outside accustomed social roles to meet one another."[188] In doing so, hybrid performance forms put "identities into play without solidifying them,"[189] thereby acknowledging that identity is not static; we constantly create and perform it.[190] In the words of Judith Butler:

> The moment in which one's staid and usual cultural perceptions fail, when one cannot with surety read the body that one sees, is precisely the moment when one is no longer sure whether the body encountered is that of a man or a woman. The vacillation between categories itself constitutes the experience of the body in question. When such categories come into question, the reality of gender is also put into crisis: it becomes unclear how to distinguish the real from the unreal....Although this insight in itself does not constitute a political revolution, no political revolution is possible without a radical shift in one's notion of the possible and the real.[191]

Hybrid performance forms have the potential to destabilize categories and modes of perception. However, as dramaturg Katherine Profeta writes, it's not clear if hybrid forms resist power structures "as a delicious ambiguity when those structures would prefer firm categorization" or if they are "evidence of those same structures' dominance, with admixture understood as an inevitable byproduct of one cultural form asserting its might over another."[192]

Two examples of hybrid form outside of The Bridge Project include choreographers Ralph Lemon's "value talks" and Meg Stuart's *Auf den Tisch!* Lemon's value talks were "a series of private conversations organized by Lemon in 2013 and 2014 at the Museum of Modern Art in New York, in which he asked artists, writers, scholars, and curators to consider how and why we talk about the value and acquisition of ephemeral works of art."[193] These talks "opened up alternatives to the conventional scholarly formats of the symposium or lecture; rather than taking these presentational devices as a given, these projects made possible the option of embodying and enacting ideas in other performative formats."[194] The talks addressed "the ephemeral nature of conversation itself: How might discussions that occur in private—about art, race, money, community, and power—be circulated without either compromising their intimacy or promising unmediated access."[195]

Meg Stuart's *Auf den Tisch*! (2009), which happened in many cities around the world, including San Francisco, is "an improvised conference about improvisation that also reflects on its own conditions" in which "performers and the audience sit at a large, square table with four microphones:"

> The performers improvise, sing, play, dance and speak; the transition from speaking and doing is blurred and arguments change their form. It's not just about acting, but also about being sensitive and listening to others. In the process, the border between the performers and the audience becomes hazy; they perform on the stage—on the table, in fact—but also next to it. Thus the conference turns into a collaboration or negotiation in which everyone brings something to the table and everyone works through the resulting situations together.[196]

Awareness of Lemon and Stuart's hybrid forms underscored my interest in cultivating hybrid performance forms in the Bay Area. Hybrid forms and in particular forms that weave critical thinking and dance have been a mainstay of The Bridge Project. Examples include *Reorganizing Ourselves* (2015), a cross-disciplinary collaboration among choreographer Deborah Hay, philosopher Alva Noë, and curator Michèle Steinwald featuring performative lectures and a performative community discussion; *Ordinary Practices of the Radical Body* (2017), a performance lecture by Monique Jenkinson and Judith Butler; *a.u.l.e.* (2017), Julie Tolentino's performance installation that embedded live blogging between two writers, Debra Levine and Scot Nakagawa, into the performance; and Netta Yerushalmy's *Paramodernities* (2018), a series of experiments deconstructing iconic dances and pairing them with scholarly lectures.

Critics have noted the power inherent in these hybrid forms. Rob Avila, reviewing *Ordinary Practices of the Radical Body*, part of the 2017 *Radical Movements* program, described that work as follows:

> The evening served up an accessible and stimulating blend of sophisticated queer theory and radical politics alongside personal anecdote and a modest but sincere lovefest across the disciplinary divide.... There was an unspoken but palpable sense of disorientation, along with the slightly giddy wonder at what might happen, when two mutually admiring representatives of two mutually exclusive worlds (art and academe, for short) let their respective guards down.[197]

CASE STUDIES
PARAMODERNITIES

In 2017, The Bridge Project presented choreographer Netta Yerushalmy's *Paramodernities*, a series of multidisciplinary lecture-performances or dance-experiments that Yerushalmy and her collaborators generated through deconstructions of landmark modern choreographies, performed alongside contributions by writers who situated these iconic works and artists within the larger project of modernism. The Bridge Project produced the West Coast premiere of three of the project's installments—those dedicated to Vaslav Nijinsky, Alvin Ailey, and Merce Cunningham.

Paramodernities was a unique hybrid of academic conference, dance performance, and town hall gathering that excavated "the canon of modern dance in radical, reverent, and violent ways" to spark new choreographies, ideas, and conversations."[198] Critic David Moreno, in his review of *Paramodernities*, noted how the work's hybrid form effectively "deconstruct[ed] laissez faire naïveté of cultural assumptions" and that the "fluid unconventional performance" proved "that perception, like gender, is multifaceted."[199] Likewise, Brian Sebert noted of *Paramodernities*:

It's not easy to say what "Paramodernities" is. It's the kind of work that keeps asking the question of itself—not implicitly but verbally, because each section is centered on one or two scholars who deliver something like a lecture. At the same time, there are dancers onstage, and what they are doing is not exactly a demonstration.[200]

When I asked Netta Yerushalmy to reflect on the power and potential of hybrid performance forms, she wrote:

> With the understanding that when we say "hybrid performance" we mean interdisciplinary work, it seems to me that work of this kind is, in and of itself, already concerned with simultaneity and complexity, regardless of its content. I think that there is something powerful in the very nature of this proposal. I've been cultivating versions of hybridity in my dances for a while. My works are aesthetically refined and replete with full-bodied dancing, but I'm in the business of cultivating confused hierarchies on stage. More often than not, I have produced dance performances with multiple choreographic and conceptual trajectories, often without totally reconciling their interface. This strategy furthers my aesthetic and ethical commitment to generating questions rather than answers and to elevating the perception of simultaneity. For me there is a political maneuver harbored in these inter-choreographic amalgams.
>
> These concerns got pushed much further in *Paramodernities*, which takes a deep dive into interdisciplinary-ness. I collaborated with twenty scholars and dancers to reverently and violently de-create canonic modern choreographies and their legacies. We did this by unleashing theory and dancing alongside each other on stage, the presences of dancing bodies and speaking bodies in an ever-unstable exchange of power and forms of legibility. The multiple layers of hybridity running through this project produce so much generative friction. Friction, tension, confusion, ambiguity—these are invaluable modes of perception and experience that are made possible in profound and crucial ways through hybrid performance work.[201]

dance of darkness: a performance, a conversation, a rehearsal for the future

Another case study in hybrid form is *dance of darkness: a performance, a conversation, a rehearsal for the future,* a collaboration between trans and queer theorist Jack Halberstam and performance artist boychild commissioned for The Bridge Project's *Radical Movements: Gender and Politics in Performance* in 2017. The work featured live performance by boychild interwoven with an academic lecture by Halberstam. This is how boychild described the work in the middle of the performance:

> This is a hybrid of monstrosity, of liminal space. It's a manifestation of a lecture and artist talk, a drag number, a performance, a dance piece. It's a lot of things and not anything. Being open to that will help you take this journey with us. This is queer theater.[202]

Halberstam opened the performance by saying, "we want to converse with each other in the grammar of dance, gesture, language, silence and images about the very original and peculiar dance repertoire that Tosh as boychild has put together for us."[203] The triangulation of Halberstam as scholar presenting his "discovered" subject, boychild presenting their talents as spectacle, and the isolated, voyeuristic audience "gave the event an odd kind of dialogic movement" that both reinstated roles and also challenged them.[204] Below are edited excerpts from *dance of darkness*:

Jack Halberstam: Let's turn to how the body works in boychild's work. One of the ways in which I understand this form of embodiment is radical illegibility. We saw this movement in and out of visibility earlier that Tosh performed for us. The body does not want to be known in this performance. It wants to hold on to being unknowable. It pulls from the viewer a kind of radical uncertainty about what it is that we're watching. It's partly why we share in the instability, the trembling and shaking landscape. We've been reading some [Gilles] Deleuze and [Félix] Guattari together, and really like their injunction to "bring something incomprehensible into the world."[205] I wanted to ask Tosh about illegibility. I don't actually want to say "ambiguity," because ambiguity expresses a sense of bothness, that there's two things that Tosh is merging, when I think illegibility is actually much more radical. Political theorist James Scott suggests that illegibility is a very underused mode towards political autonomy.[206] Instead, we tend to focus on being visible, and we think that that's the way to become powerful, is to be visible. But that means that we're not looking at the immense power that is located in illegibility.

boychild: I like illegibility so much better than ambiguity. I don't want to be ambiguous. This is where visibility for me has even been dangerous. It's like, "Oh, shit, do they see me? Oh, shit, do they see me?" Airports are places where you kind of want to be as invisible as possible when you're trans. They have these really scary backrooms in airports where they pretend not to speak English.

JH: When we talk about transgenderism, there's a sense that we want to know who is a man and who is a woman when in fact what we really want to do is mess up those categories and inscribe a kind of illegibility across embodiment. Illegibility is one of the things that I feel your work performs.

bc: I like the idea of illegibility. I'm placing things in liminal ways, thinking about shadow or light as medium, going back to that place formally and integrating that with theater, all these crisscrossing ways.

JH: We want to end with a different understanding of the politics of the radical body. Too many times politics today is about knowing the body, who I am. In one song that boychild uses, it says: "I am, I am, I am," but there was no finish to that sentence. There is just a sense of becoming, repeating, going on. This idea of being in bodies that are not clear to each other and that remain incomprehensible offers us another way towards the political. boychild is not simply something other, a kind of extraordinary otherness that we watch with rapt attention. They are also someone who reflects our being back to us in fragmented form. He is not simply a mirror, but a mirrored surface that is made of multiple fragments. To look at boychild is yourself to become fragmentary and to recognize your own total disintegration.[207]

Katherine Profeta cautions that "many histories of racial and cultural hybridity are impossible to celebrate, woven as they are throughout with theft and violence."[208] Mindful of these histories, if curators can commission and support processes between artistic equals where mutual respect marks the collaboration, hybrid forms have potential to subvert and shift outdated approaches to identity and open up new territory for performance. Just as the architecture of cultural organizations must evolve to reflect cultural equity values, so too must the structure of performance itself.

Chapter 6

Expanding the Canon

history
many histories
and these histories
all act on each other

what are the histories?
they wind together to make the present and then everyone sees it
everyone sees it from a completely different point of view
a completely different view

—Simone Forti, performing her "News Animation" in Have We Come a
Long Way, Baby?, part of The Bridge Project in 2014[209]

To re-imagine the future, we must reconcile with the past. Reconciling with the past differs from repeating it. "To know a pattern is not to be forced to repeat it."[210] In the art world, our time is marked by "an upsurge of interest in memory"[211] and an "obsession with performing and redefining the past."[212] In dance, with the death of modern masters like Martha Graham, José Limón, Pina Bausch, Merce Cunningham, Trisha Brown, and Paul Taylor, legacy has become a pressing topic. In response to the loss of these foundational voices, some single-author modern dance companies have become repertory companies that mix the founder's voice with other voices. Others have undertaken explicit legacy projects, such as Stephen Petronio's *Bloodlines*. The Merce Cunningham Dance Company made the decision to disband after Cunningham died, but it continues to set repertory on other companies and lead educational programming; they recently presented a massive international series of projects honoring Cunningham's one hundredth birthday. Despite ongoing conversations about legacy in the field, dance, compared to other art forms, remains "particularly resistant to change, whether from choreographic trusts, diehard classicists, or others who fear the loss of a choreographer's legacy."[213] Often, when institutions develop practices to preserve a dance artist's legacy, these practices can take on a powerful life of their own, separate from the work itself.

Art history has long been presented in tidy, linear terms, with the assumption that culture progresses through a series of one-on-one conversations between master and student in which the master casts a long shadow of overpowering influence that their progeny must metabolize (as proposed in literary critic Harold Bloom's 1973 book, *The Anxiety of Influence: A Theory of Poetry*).[214] Likewise, art history is often framed as a neat parade of conceptual paradigms, each of which spawns the next conceptual framework in a tidy progression of "isms."

Transmission of historic dance forms enables contemporary artists to situate themselves in a progression of ideas. Dance legacies, like any form of history, are valuable archives that, in the words of poet Claudia Rankine, both "influence and challenge the definitions we construct for ourselves."[215] Yet linear paradigms of influence, as stories of successive dominance, reify the tendency, present in any lineage, for one voice to dominate others. Traditional paradigms of lineage also fail to account for the nonlinear way ideas travel through and across culture, such as laterally from peer to peer, in networks, and across disciplines. Choreographer Netta Yerushalmy, who conceived and directed *Paramodernities*, a multidisciplinary engagement with many strands of the dance canon, asks, "What does it feel like to consider the legacy as a horizontal thing and not as the chronological historicized narrative that we know?[216]

Traditional paradigms of legacy also ignore the multiplicity of identity. Transmission of ideas does not occur in a cultural vacuum, but is refracted through identities, both of the giver and the recipient.[217] Through our multiple selves, ideas splinter and hybridize. In the dance context, where transmission happens not only visually and conceptually, but also from body to body, legacy is cellular. It lives in the body in a million different pieces.

Part of shifting cultural power is expanding the canon and how we relate to it. First, as visual art curator Maura Reilly writes, we must bring in multiple voices to "comment, debate, and shape tradition."[218] Second, we must resituate choreographic transmission in multidisciplinary spaces and in spaces populated by artists who identify as coming from historically disenfranchised communities. Third, in spaces where historical dances are taught, we must make space not only for the transmission of form, but also for dialogue around identity. The identity of the author and the identity of the performer are equally important parts of the dance. Expanding our engagement with the dance canon involves valuing the subjective perception and embodiment of the original material as much as valuing the material's original conception.

In these expanded conversations with the dance canon, we must ask who is included in the canon, who is not, and why. In doing so, we cultivate consciousness about which paradigms to preserve and which to change. We also create space for critiquing the idea of canonicity itself.[219] Dance critic Brian Sebert, in his review of Netta Yerushalmy's *Paramodernities*, asks us:

> Who has the right to dance what?
> Is a legacy public and what can legitimately be done to it?
> What do staged bodies signify, other than mere form?[220]

CASE STUDIES
HAVE WE COME A LONG WAY, BABY?

The Bridge Project first considered canon in 2014 with *Have We Come a Long Way, Baby?* This program did not challenge legacy, but honored it through an intergenerational lineup featuring the work of white postmodern choreographers. This was before I started removing my own work from The Bridge Project programming. Dance critic Heather Desaulniers called it "a phenomenal celebration of West Coast post-modern dance, bringing together four powerhouse choreographers in a single program."[221] Anna Halprin, age ninety-four at the time, performed her solo, *The Courtesan and the Crone*; Simone Forti, age eighty, performed her *News Animations*; Peiling Kao, age thirty-nine, performed a solo that I made for her called *soft(is)hard*; and I, age forty-two, performed Lucinda Child's *Carnation*. In the face of a long history of framing New York as the epicenter of postmodernism, I wanted to organize an intergenerational program around Anna Halprin, rooted on the West

Coast, who taught so many postmodern pioneers, including Forti, who noted during the post-show discussion:

> Among the things I learned from Anna Halprin was to trust my body and to have kinesthetic awareness so that I'm aware of what my body wants to do in the moment, and I can transmit that. I never got caught up in the "turnout" and the "holding your stomach in." When I met Anna, we would forget the textbooks. She would ask us what we most wondered about. And then we would talk about what we most wondered about. And then she would suggest certain reading that might be in the general area of what we were wondering about. We were exploring things, we were experimenting.[222]

Have We Come a Long Way, Baby? was a meditation on postmodern dance lineage through the female body. In a post-show discussion, moderator and dance historian Janice Ross said:

> You could look at what you saw tonight as history, as snapshots from the archive, but I think it was also a lens for the present moment. One of the things these pieces in particular highlight for me is the frankness about the female body onstage. I think that the Judson Dance Theater was about presenting a new image of the female body. Beyond that frankness of the female body, it was also the repudiation of deforming the body through training practices. It addressed the body where it was with kindness and gentleness. Tonight you saw task refracted through women's labor. Lucinda Childs plays with that a lot in *Carnation*—with the mundane tasks with the sponges and hair curlers. Also it was present in the real labor that Simone Forti was using in *News Animations* and Anna Halprin's play with undressing in *The Courtesan and the Crone*.[223]

All of the female choreographers featured in *Have We Come a Long Way, Baby?* were white. Although the program presented an intergenerational feminist perspective on lineage, the program's feminism was not intersectional with regard to race. The only woman of color on the program was Peiling Kao. In putting together this book, I asked Kao about what it was like to be on the program:

Hope Mohr: What kind of perspective on lineage did the program give you?

Peiling Kao: Female choreographer in American postmodern dance perspective.

HM: You were the only artist of color on the program. Did you think about race in the context of the program? Or the intersection of race and female identity?

PK: No, I did not think about race in the context of the program. Now that you're asking, I'm curious about why I did not.

HM: Any other reflections on your experience in the program?

PK: I felt honored to be involved and share the stage with these important female icons in American postmodern dance.[224]

In hindsight, it's striking how absent race was from not only my mind, but also Peiling's. I easily could have made the program's feminism more intersectional—for example, by casting a woman of color to perform Lucinda Child's solo, rather than myself, or featuring the work of the many outstanding female choreographers of color who have studied with Anna Halprin. But in 2014, these ideas did not occur to me. Although I was well-versed in the theory of intersectionality as a law student and as an activist, I had not yet put these ideas into curatorial practice. As a curator, I was still operating in the limited ambit of my experience as a dancer, which was bounded by the white postmodern world. It was as if focusing on the female postmodern experience precluded me from also thinking about race.

TEN ARTISTS RESPOND TO "LOCUS"

In 2016, with my increasing awareness of the need for a more intersectional, multidisciplinary approach to dance history, The Bridge Project presented *Ten Artists Respond to "Locus,"* which commissioned ten Bay Area artists to learn Trisha Brown's iconic 1975 *Locus* from Diane Madden, Co-Artistic Director of the Trisha Brown Dance Company, and make new work in response. *Ten Artists Respond to "Locus"* project was part of the Trisha Brown Dance Company's renewed commitment to sharing Brown's legacy with a broader audience.

Traditionally, choreographic transmission of Brown's work has occurred from body to body for the sake of replicating the dance with as much historical fidelity as possible. The *Locus* project posed new questions: How do you transmit a historical work of art to inspire contemporary authorship, as opposed to transmission to inspire allegiance to the original? How do you transmit a work of art in such a way that allows artists from different backgrounds and disciplines to engage with the form on their own terms? These are questions not only of structure and resources, but also of pedagogy, ethics, and aesthetics.

Identity was a part of all of the commissioned responses to *Locus*, even in the white artists' work, whether they were aware of it or not. In reflections that I invited the commissioned artists to write after the project was over, it became clear that issues of identity were at play throughout the creative process.[225] But I did not make explicit time and space within the frame of the project for the participating artists to discuss how their identities impacted their experience of engaging with Brown's work. As the *Locus* project organizer, I chose to take a hands-off approach to questions of cultural and racial identity in order to avoid interfering with the process of choreographic transmission and the participating artists' processes. In retrospect I see my "neutrality" as complacency—a curatorial blind spot.

Curators are a kind of witness and there is an ethics of witness. As a white witness, I am not neutral; I must be accountable to my own humanity and the humanity of others. Scholar Christina Sharpe refers to the "violence of abstraction" in relationship to the African American experience,[226] indicating that in some contexts, abstraction can be dehumanizing. I wrote the following after the *Locus* project was over:

> As curators, we can't take the neutrality of abstraction for granted. How can curators make dialogue about cultural identity essential not only in the context of presenting artists of color, but also for white artists, so that whiteness is no longer the default cultural perspective?[227]

Throughout the *Locus* project, I thought about the need for dialogue about identity, but I felt there wasn't enough time. Diane Madden and I discussed using improvisational practice in relationship to Brown's source material as a way to bring in and honor participant subjectivity and embodiment; however, we felt that time constraints prevented us from fully utilizing this essential tool.

So often there's a sense that there's not enough time. I want to resist the logic of scarcity as the basis for curatorial decisions. Since the *Locus* project, I have committed to making time to cultivate the conditions for all artists to bring their full selves to the table. This commitment has informed how I have structured curatorial projects since (for example, by building in time for social gatherings and informal discussions among artists, rather than assuming it will happen on people's own time), and also how I facilitate my own choreographic process (for example, making time for people to check in at the beginning of rehearsal—even if it's a short rehearsal and the dance needs a ton of work and the show is in three days).

Part of shifting cultural power is resisting the traps of urgency and scarcity. Part of putting cultural equity into practice is insisting on slowing down so everyone can show up. In rooms where we teach and make dance, how can we make time to honor the subjective experience of the dancer who receives the information as much as we honor the teacher?

SIGNALS FROM THE WEST: BAY AREA ARTISTS IN CONVERSATION WITH MERCE CUNNINGHAM AT 100

In 2017, I received emails from Brenda Way, Artistic Director of ODC, and from Claudia La Rocco, Editor-in-Chief of SFMOMA's Open Space, both asking if The Bridge Project would be interested in partnering with their institutions and the Merce Cunningham Trust to co-produce an event in conjunction with the one hundredth anniversary of Merce Cunningham's birth. I had a personal connection to Cunningham's work, having trained on scholarship at the Cunningham studio for over a year as a young dancer in New York. I was thrilled about a new opportunity to re-engage with dance lineage in an experimental way and to apply the lessons I had learned from the *Locus* program.

Signals from the West: Bay Area Artists in Conversation with Merce Cunningham at 100 was a multidisciplinary exchange co-produced by The Bridge Project, SFMOMA's Open Space, ODC Theater, and the Merce Cunningham Trust as part of an international celebration of the one hundredth year of Cunningham's birth. The project commissioned works by ten Bay Area artists from many different disciplines in response to the choreographer's legacy, presented in tandem with excerpts of Cunningham repertory performed by Bay Area dancers. *Signals from the West* also included *Inherited Bodies*, an evening of lecture-demonstrations by four Bay Area dance artists responding to the prompt: How do you reconcile, honor, and resist the past? I co-curated the entire project along with Claudia La Rocco, Director of Community Engagement at SFMOMA, and Julie Potter, Director of ODC Theater.

Signals from the West was the first time Cunningham's choreography had ever been taught in a multidisciplinary setting in order to facilitate the authorship of new work. Lead teaching artists and former Cunningham company dancers Silas Riener and Rashaun Mitchell talked about how they had "no blueprint" and "no model for how to proceed" in this context.[228] The residency was also an experiment for the commissioned artists, who entered a conversation with Cunningham's work and with each other, tasked with responding to an icon at a time when traditional canons are being rethought.

The commissioned artists included, in addition to choreographers, a poet/playwright, sound artists, visual artists, writers, and performance artists. As co-curators, we intentionally convened a cohort of artists that was not majority white. In order to ensure that the process offered participating artists ample time to explore and discuss issues relating to identity in the context of engaging with Cunningham's work, we held a series of artist potlucks months ahead of the residency that began the studio process. We designed these potlucks to create space and time for the artists to get to know each other. We also wanted the potlucks to frame *Signals from the West* as a place of experimentation where the artists were encouraged to ask big questions about identity, canon, and culture. Six months ahead of the residency, my co-curators and I offered the artists this prompt at our first potluck:

> – How do you feel you are or are not in conversation with the past in your work? The past could be artistic, familial, geographic, and/or political.[229]

At the second artist potluck, two months ahead of the residency, we watched video of Cunningham's work and discussed the following prompts:

> – What questions, tensions, or curiosities come up for you in watching Cunningham's work?
> – What questions of form?
> – What questions of identity?[230]

At this potluck, I shared lessons I had learned from the *Locus* project. I was transparent about how *Signals from the West* would require the co-curators to balance the different needs of participating dancers, commissioned artists, teaching artists, and producing partners; how it surfaced both questions of identity and questions of form; and how we as co-curators hoped the artists would approach it not as a gig, but as an opportunity to work in new ways, whether that meant collaborating with another commissioned artist or simply working in a different way than they had previously. We framed the project as both a group process and an individual process.

We also framed the project as two conversations: first, a conversation between the artist and Merce Cunningham's work (responding to source material) and second, a conversation between the individual artist and the other artists in the room (collaborating). At the second artist potluck, we asked the artists the following questions:

- How might your interests and needs be different in each of these two conversations?
- How can you make the most out of each conversation?
- What conditions allow you to be vulnerable in a group creative process?

The artist potlucks cultivated a sense of permission to ask big questions such as: Why is Cunningham relevant? Can he still be relevant? Why bother? These questions are essential if we're going to engage with the dance canon because many artists don't see any reason to do so. In response to the project's culminating performances, artist Leena Joshi wrote about *Signals from the West* for SFMOMA's Open Space:

These days I'm mostly disinterested in the white male canon—a decision I made in order to make more decisions, to feel that I had agency in discovering for me rather than for the sake of an institution.[231]

After the artist potlucks, the commissioned artists and a handful of Bay Area dancers selected from an audition gathered with Riener and Mitchell for a two-week residency. Riener and Mitchell were there primarily to offer the source material of Cunningham's work through teaching technique class, showing and discussing video from the Cunningham Trust archive, and leading the group in a series of exercises modeled on various chance procedures that Cunningham used to compose his work. They offered intensive coaching of the dancers, but declined to cross the line from transmission to mentorship with regard to the commissioned artists. In an email, Mitchell wrote:

As far as the individual artists' process is concerned, I don't think [mentorship of the commissioned artists] is necessarily our purview. We haven't commissioned them after all. I think our focus and role is to facilitate practice and dialogue around Merce's ideas. What the artists decide to do with that is up to them.[232]

The residency encouraged "a critical, probing engagement with Cunningham, one befitting the artist's own restless disposition."[233] Co-curator La Rocco described how the residency was a space for destabilizing and expanding the canon:

When someone's anointed part of the canon, what was vibrant and uneasy can become codified, it can calcify. The sense I got from being [present in the

Signals residency] was a bunch of smart individuals poking something, flipping it over, looking at it upside down—and not just recreating a piece. It's an experiment.[234]

Once the residency began, we continued to support critical thinking by ending each week of the residency with an open studio and salon, which invited the general public to come watch the artists at work and to engage with all of the artists in discussion about the process.

Part of what made the *Signals* residency so effective in going beyond traditional approaches to dance history was that throughout the residency, the transmission of historical dances for the repertory dancers occurred in the same space and at the same time as exercises for the commissioned artists designed to generate new material. This literal proximity allowed various aspects of Cunningham's work—its formal vocabularies, its compositional structures, its archive, its sociopolitical context—to rub up against each other. This, in combination with the generosity of Riener and Mitchell's facilitation, allowed competing desires to occupy the room: a dancer's desire to practice repertory shared space with a commissioned artist writing or witnessing; commissioned artists who wanted to collaborate shared space with other commissioned artists who wanted to work solo. Artists could move among different modes of engaging with the source material on their own terms.

The first week of the *Signals* residency, the group shared a morning warm-up. Having trained dancers in the room modeled an at-homeness in the body that invited everyone, including people without a formal physical practice, to have an embodied experience. Riener and Mitchell alternated improvisation with traditional Cunningham exercises and brought in aspects of their own practice, which observes and responds to external stimuli as well as the internal landscape of the body. Day one began with an exploration of walking as a starting point for making choices about direction, speed, facing, rhythm, posture, and style. ("Walk formally. Now walk informally.") Two subsequent days began with all participating movers, including myself, creating spinal pathways while seated, a somatic exercise that eventually moved into the Cunningham spinal lexicon: curve, arch, twist, and tilt. Riener and Mitchell guided the group through increasingly complex movements.

At the time of the *Signals* residency, Cunningham's notes on his methods for creating specific dances had only recently become available (albeit on a restricted basis). Access to a wealth of such archival materials allows people, in the words of Dazaun Soleyn, to hear Cunningham's "voice through the notes and the compositional systems."[235] Several of the commissioned artists noted that direct access to the archive humanized Cunningham and his dances.

Often, as commissioned artist Maxe Crandall put it, "tradition means erasing" and "lineages are cleaned up."[236] But in this residency, the group talked openly about the fallibility of the work—how it was and remains radical in some ways, but not in others. For example, Riener told us that although "there were tons of queer people around and there was acceptance of that, the assignment of parts and the partnering was very binary in terms of gender."[237] Cunningham's work parallels the way in which Judson Dance Theater democratized the body, but not the field. I found it odd that in his notes for *Fielding Sixes* (1980), Cunningham refers to himself in the third person. (For instance: "Merce Cunningham would then roll the dice for position in the space.") Does this reflect an egotistical belief in his inevitable legacy? Or a disconnection from the self? As Danishta Rivero said, "I have a much better appreciation for his work because I see all those parts that are a bit messy and contradictory."[238]

For the Merce Cunningham Trust, a vital question is: How to balance fidelity to legacy with the permission to leave aspects of that work behind? When contemporary artists want to shift the work from its original state, how far is too far? As the artists worked in response to the archive, questions arose about whether the identity of the work was in the body, in the compositional system, or somewhere in between. Does Cunningham's work reside, as dance critic Joan Acocella says, "in the dancers and their specific way of moving, or does it lie in the dances themselves, if such a thing can be conceived of in art that has no original texts?"[239] Extracting the body from a choreographic legacy can make the work accessible to artists from different disciplines. But if we extract Cunningham's work from the body, is it still his work?

The commissioned artists entered this project with varying degrees of opposition to the specter of the white male genius. Many had a sense that Cunningham's work was "inaccessible," as commissioned artist Sophia Wang argued, or something they had always "experienced from afar," as commissioned artist Dazaun Soleyn observed.[240] Commissioned artist Christy Funsch recounted that when she took class at the Cunningham studio in New York City, she "never felt like she belonged" and that the whole idea of lineage made her "panic a little, as if I have to measure up to all who have lived and made before."[241]

The combination of the artist potlucks preceding the residency and the friendly environment of the residency, made possible through the artists' generosity and responsiveness, diffused some understandable tensions. Politics did not loudly enter the room. Riener, in an interview for SFMOMA's Open Space with La Rocco at the end of the project, noted:

> At the end of the day, all of the people in that [residency] agreed to do this project. So on some level, they were already past...concerns over whether their communities or peers wouldn't understand why they're engaging in the work of a dead white man. At the end of the day, this is a moral question that everyone has to answer according to your sense of yourself as an artist and your career trajectory. These ten artists wanted to engage, even if it was outside of their comfort zone or outside of their knowledge, they wanted to be there. Or at least, were willing to do it and to be able to have an opportunity to show their work.[242]

In that same interview, LaRocco asked Mitchell and Riener about the ways in which working with such a wide range of artists in the residency "was liberating, or the ways in which it was stymying."[243] Mitchell responded:

> It was liberating in the actual exchange with people in the moment. Leading up to it, there were so many unknowns and I would say it was much more stressful to imagine how it would play out? And to prepare for the different eventualities; how to keep one person engaged and challenged while another person is entering from a much more novice level. But in the end—and I want to say that this is specific to the Bay Area or to the culture there—it wasn't an issue at all. In fact, everyone came with such openness and such willingness to move across their own border lines, you know?[244]

Riener and Mitchell's fluency and comfort with conversations about cultural identity defined the residency environment. As Riener stated:

> I felt really ready [in the *Signals* residency] to have identity politics conversations and whiteness conversations around this work. Partly because those are interesting conversations to have, and those conversations have not really been had around Merce's work because it's all swathed in the protection of abstraction somehow, which is really being dismantled right now in a very important way.[245]

Mitchell acknowledged that there are many ways to provide an expanded context for repertory:

You can do that in subtle ways, you can do that periodically, you can do that in a big, grand gesture. There's lots of different ways to do that. I think it puts people at ease to know exactly where you stand as the transmitter of this knowledge, and that you also are aware of all of the other questions and critiques that are going on.[246]

On the one hand, the friendly, nonconfrontational atmosphere of the residency encouraged exploration—there is something to be said for creating a sanctuary for artists to set aside political struggles. On the other hand, does any creative process stand outside the messiness of the world? Art critic Aruna D'Souza has asserted that there can be "no fiction of the autonomous realm" in art: "Institutions either have to actively work to dismantle racism, or they are reinforcing it."[247] The body and its techniques are "never abstract, but rather ineluctably located within a historical moment and a cultural/political system."[248]

After the residency, the *Signals from the West* artists had a two-and-a-half-month period of creating work in conversation with the experience. I was curious how they would respond to the dusty archetype of the artist as the lone hero making their mark. I was curious what counter-narratives would arise— perhaps that of the artist simultaneously marking the world and being marked by it. Perhaps the archetype of a group of artists in conversation with each other and the world.

Artist and writer Leena Joshi reflected on the program's culminating performances and installations:

Before attending *Signals from the West*, I knew very little about Merce Cunningham, and what I now know I've gleaned from witnessing a group of dancers and artists traveling through the prism that is his legacy, beaming out something new and spilling it across the walls and screen and floor. It was probably the best way for me to decide to care; to be given the opportunity to absorb the intention and structure of Cunningham's pedagogy of dance through a group of people who explicitly and implicitly deal in the arduous, messy existence that is *today*, not just *yesterday*.[249]

As one of the program's curators, I felt like *Signals from the West* was a success for many reasons. First, it was not an exercise in nostalgia, but an in-depth process of bringing artists together for meaningful collaboration and exchange over a long period of time to make new work. Second, the process built collaborative relationships between artists that have outlasted the project. Third, we as co-curators insisted on building in enough time into the process for personal discussions that allowed each artist to bring their full selves to the room.

Beyond the process, the resulting installations and performances were bold, vibrant, personal, and widely varied in terms of tone, discipline, content, and format. Each of the commissioned works responded to a different aspect of Cunningham's works, which threw Cunningham's legacy into new light. Many of the commissioned works challenged the presumed neutrality of abstract white male art and explored how the artist's identities collided with Cunningham's compositional methods. The process and its results showed how dance can engage with form and be socially engaged at the same time.

Chapter 7

Reckoning with Aesthetics

CURATORIAL AND FUNDING PRACTICES: TROUBLING THE SINGULAR STANDARD

Susan Sontag wrote that "good taste" is "always a repressive standard when invoked by institutions."[250] Institutional cultural power and aesthetic judgment go hand in hand. How can curators and funders evaluate what "good" dance is without imposing some form of repression? For hundreds of years, artistic excellence and merit have been measured according to the values of the Western European tradition. Criteria like "craft," "mastery," and "virtuosity" often work as codewords for art that conforms to Western European, patriarchal, hetero-sexist norms.[251] The dominance of the Western European art tradition has rel-egated many artists to "second-class status": dance that is deemed utilitarian, popular, "ethnic," "street," and/or socially engaged is underrated, under-re-sourced, and excluded from support and visibility.[252]

In a field with a diversity of forms and traditions, the concept of a single standard of artistic excellence is not useful. There are many different kinds of artistic excellence. We must evaluate a work of art within its specific cultural context. Who was the work made for? Why did the artist create it? Answers to these questions should influence the criteria we use to evaluate artistic value. Ashley Montagu wrote, "all cultures must be judged in relation to their own history, and all individuals and groups in relation to their cultural history, and definitely not by the arbitrary standard of any single culture."[253] We should not evaluate a ballet and a hula using standards developed for ballet. We must evaluate ballet based on our knowledge of other ballet and evaluate hula based on our knowledge of other hula. Only by seeing many hula dances might someone be in a position to ask whether a particular hula is better than other hulas.

One example (among countless) of the erasure and damage that happens when white people apply a singular aesthetic to all forms of dance occurred when white dance critic Allan Ulrich reviewed Gerald Casel's commissioned response to Trisha Brown's *Locus* as part of The Bridge Project in 2016, *Ten Artists Respond to "Locus."* Ulrich wrote in his review:

> What binds Gerald Casel's "Taglish" to [Trisha] Brown remains a mystery, but the choreographer and Suzette Sagisi provided some of the fleetest dancing of the evening. Casel notes that the piece represents tensions between Filipino and American culture, but his finely crafted mirror duet was satisfying in itself.[254]

Casel responded to Ulrich as follows:

> [Ulrich's] writing misses the mark altogether, even glossing over the tension between Filipino and American culture. He instead focuses on what he deems legible and worthy of affirming: the mirror duet. The fact that his white, male gaze cannot register any of the elements that portrayed voguing embodied in my whirling effeminate gestures, the traditional Filipino folk dance, and the blending of vernacular and postmodern dance underscores his incapacity to include other forms of dance beyond his narrow definition. Ulrich's response sheds a light on the invisibility of colored folks' culture to mainstream dance criticism that privilege Western and Eurocentric dance forms and unfortunately perpetuates the mechanisms of coloniality. In dance criticism, words, like actions, have power. When critics use (or do not use) words to describe culture beyond white space, they basically ignore and in effect, erase, the culture they think they describe.[255]

Engaging multiple voices from different artistic traditions in the process of evaluating art helps to ensure that a range of questions are asked.

In order to move away from using a singular standard for evaluating artistic excellence, white funders, critics, and curators must "question, mark, and check"[256] how white aesthetic traditions create implicit bias. If we have no knowledge of a particular form, we should not use our existing knowledge as a substitute for standards of which we are ignorant. People who lack knowledge about a given dance form need to do their homework before evaluating its merits. Performer and dance scholar Charmian Wells responded to a Gia Kourlas review of a DanceAfrica performance:

> Let me be clear, I am not suggesting that only black critics can review dances of the African diaspora. The central issue in this review is a glaring lack of cultural literacy combined with a lack of self-awareness about this deficiency, any sense of the historical role of racism in US concert dance criticism, and a galling sense of authority over subject matter with which the reviewer is clearly unfamiliar. Nor did she take it upon herself to ask questions or do research.[257]

If we want to avoid using limited or biased standards of artistic excellence, what questions can we ask to evaluate if a dance is good? At a 2019 public gathering as part of *Dancing Around Race*, lead artist Gerald Casel asked guest speaker, scholar, and artist Thomas DeFrantz, "How do you know when a dance is good?" DeFrantz responded:

> This idea of valuing [art] has to do with who is doing the valuing and what's it towards.... What is the creative encounter pitched or tilted towards? In that encounter or exchange, then we can decide whether the art is helping make something possible.... Who are we offering the work to? Is the thing doing what needs to be done in the moment?... It's hard because white supremacy and colonialism—these structures of oppression and domination—keep trying to refer us to the outside, like it matters if we're not on the stage at an opera house. We know it doesn't, but what we haven't figured out, especially as people of color making work, is how do we value our address to our family.... I think when we can start to understand how we're compelled to make or be involved in the arts, and then face that out, like who is it facing toward? Then we can start answering these questions of value, care, quality, if that's a vector that someone wants to live in, like is it a good dance? What can the dance do? Can the dance help make a communication shift or help make something possible?[258]

In order to shift cultural power, we can look beyond signifiers such as mastery and virtuosity. Here are other possibilities:

- Is the work authentic? Does it have cultural integrity?
- Does the work promote freedom?
- Is it necessary or urgent?

- Does it positively impact the community?
- Does it promote joy and pleasure?
- Is it relevant or contemporary?
- Does it make me feel something?
- Does the artist succeed in communicating their intention?
- What does the work risk?
- Was there reciprocity in the creative process between the artist and the community?

Funders and curators have begun to trouble the idea of a singular standard for artistic excellence. New frameworks for talking about aesthetics include the "Aesthetic Perspectives" framework developed by Animating Democracy, now applied by the MAP Fund, a philanthropic arts organization that has an explicit commitment to supporting work that "challenges canon and convention and, by extension, ableist, cis, heteronormative, Western cultural dominance."[259] Adopting evaluation criteria and funding structures that explicitly prioritize cultural equity have concrete impacts on artist experience seeking support as well as on funding outcomes.[260] In 2016, the Sustainable Arts Foundation made the public announcement that at least half of their awards would go to applicants of color.[261] Following this public announcement, the percentage of applicants of color to the Sustainable Arts Foundation increased from twenty percent to over forty-one percent.[262]

The performance of white benevolence has become the norm in the arts, especially in the wake of the 2020 killing of George Floyd. The "fetishization" of artists of color has "consumed the current moment."[263] How can our cultural equity work be less reactive and less about showing other people how "woke" we are? How can we deepen our critical thinking around artistic value to include multiple perspectives?

CHOREOGRAPHIC PRACTICE: SUMMONING POETIC NERVE
A BODY IN THE WORLD

As a white choreographer-curator, the most personal political work that I can do is to reckon with my own aesthetics. What does it mean for my commitment to cultural equity to permeate my own artmaking? There's no territory that feels more personal than the politics of my own imagination.

How can I imagine beyond what I know?

Curating, as a practice of critical thinking, expands the horizon of what I know and therefore of what I can imagine. Curating constantly recontextualizes my choreographic methods, priorities, preferences, and orientation. As a curator, I try to present dances that are not in line with my taste. If I think a dance is too difficult, too messy, too edgy, too ambiguous, too unprofessional, or too long, that's an opportunity for self-reflection. These standards hold unspoken politics.

But curating dance and making dance are different. How I make dance feels deeper than language. As a choreographer, I have to reckon with a subterranean, ancient layer of myself that easily hides in the intellectual realm of curating. What comes out of my own body? How does my personality show up in the dance studio for collaborators? How do I engage with dancers in generating movement? What is the racial composition of ensembles that I hire? Even if I am working with a diverse cast, am I nonetheless imposing white assumptions of artistic value on the ensemble? Do my politics say one thing and my dances another? Does my own choreography do what I think it does? Does my personal choreographic practice square with what I say to colleagues on a grant panel about another artists' work?

The impossibility of removing my body from the world is my point of departure for a liberatory aesthetics. As a young dancer, I was drawn to classical technique because, as a physical practice, it offered me the possibility of burnishing my body. But there was never any chance of me escaping myself. It—and the world—always found a way in. Where the body is the medium (and when is it not?), withdrawing the world from the art, or the art from the world, is a fiction.

Virginia Woolf, in *A Room of One's Own*, reflects that Shakespeare's mind was "free and unimpeded" because he was a man and therefore had no "desire to protest, to preach, to proclaim an injury, to pay off a score, to make the world the witness of some hardship or grievance."[264] A "free and unimpeded" mind may sound tempting. But as a female in a sexist culture, locating and trusting my voice continues to be an essential and valuable struggle. My body, in contact with the world, is a source of wisdom. As liberation psychology insists, our lived experience must be the starting point of ethical reflection.[265]

Being in dialogue with the world sometimes paralyzes me or overwhelms my ability to make art. Faced with the heavy legacy of white privilege in the arts, I sit often with the question of whether to stop making dances altogether. Author Jess Row talks about similar questions facing white writers:

[T]he question of whether to write at all is one white writer should take seriously. To produce art—even explicitly anti-racist art—under conditions that reward white subjectivity, center it, and render it harmless and neutral, is, arguably, a way of collaborating with and sustaining those conditions. This is a case where the argument that "the solution to the problems within the work of art is to produce more art" may actually be the root of the problem. Because it may be that white writers can never escape the horror of performing within the family romance of whiteness and the white state. It maybe that [the] choice is to have no more performances at all, but just to resume ordinary life, which for the artist is a kind of death.... The real point...for me...[is] not to die but to go on living in a new key."[266]

As a choreographer, how do I live in a new key?

A DIALOGIC PROCESS

If I want to make dance that liberates me and other people, I need to summon what Adrienne Rich calls "poetic nerve."[267] Poetic nerve means engaging in a dialogic process, not a self-absorbed process, with material, collaborators, and the world. This is the choreographic corollary of decentering the curator. Hilton Als critiqued Young Jean Lee's play *Straight White Men* by saying, "she's made a 'white' play: shallow, soporific, *and all about itself*" (emphasis mine).[268] Finding our poetic nerve requires us to step outside ourselves in order to see from other people's perspectives.

As a white, privileged person, poetic nerve requires me to see the world not from the center, but from the edge—to see with what Rich calls an "outsider's eye:"

It was only when I could finally affirm the outsider's eye as the source of a legitimate and coherent vision, that I began to be able to do the work I truly wanted to do, live the kind of life I truly wanted to live, instead of carrying out the assignments I had been given as a privileged woman.[269]

Seeing with an outsider's eye means seeing past my own privileged story. It means having difficult conversations with myself: Where has privilege made me lazy? Where has privilege created blind spots in my thinking? Where is my ego driving the process? Where am I shirking accountability? Rich urges poets to examine their work "for ignorance, solipsism, laziness, dishonesty, automatic writing."[270] Poetic nerve is a refusal to be comfortable.[271]

I seek out conversations and circumstances that challenge the terms on which I make a dance. When external forces destabilize my voice, I have to dig deeper for what I need to say. Choreographing in dialogue with an unfamiliar setting yields welcome surprises. I've made dances in a decrepit blacksmith shop open to the elements; in the charred landscape left by wildfires; in sculptures of liquid clay. Making dance with collaborators (especially difficult ones) always takes the work beyond where I could take it alone.

Seeing with an outsider's eye does not mean, as a white person, that I need to tell other people's stories or stop listening to my own inner voice. Poetic nerve does not mean surrendering authorship. It does not mean emotional retreat or disengagement. It means going beyond myself, and then back within again, and then again out past myself, and so on, in a constant conversation between the dance and the world. This dialogic process makes sense because my liberation is bound up with yours.

ETHICAL ABSTRACTION

The second part of poetic nerve is committing to socially engaged choreography while leaving space for the unknown. I make dance because the process is a terrifying mystery. I don't want dancemaking to feel like getting from point A to point B. When it's working, dancemaking is a process that invites parts of myself into the room that I am unready to name in daily life.

Any time I say, "this is a dance about X," I risk disavowing the mysterious part of the choreographic process. There are many pressures to make message-driven dance. Grant applications and marketing campaigns require artists to tether dances to message. Activist commitments impose additional expectations: Will the dance live up to its self-proclaimed politics? Many audiences expect a narrative or thematic through line.

A message-dominated dance can prevent a choreographer from listening within. Anchoring my choreography exclusively outside myself—in the desire to make the world a better place, for example, risks disconnection from my imagination. The painter Cornelia Parker writes:

> For me the conscious part of making a drawing is deciding on a process. What the process then releases is something else. Your unconscious mind always knows more than your conscious mind.... What you need is a catalyst to unleash that knowledge. A concept can be that catalyst or a decoy.[272]

Poetic nerve demands that I be open to material that is seemingly off-topic, surprising, and tangential. Unless I am open to my unconscious, what I make will fail to "exceed the prescribed common vocabulary."[273] It will not have what artist Paul Chan calls "good form," which "not only pushes that idea into a higher order of meaning. It also gives the material that shaped that idea a new reason to exist."[274] I don't want my political commitments to reduce my dances to overly literal expressions of will. I want to leave room for the fragment and for the mystery. When we reduce socially engaged dance to message, we reduce the potential of dance and ignore the nature of dance as a medium.

The answer, however, is not a retreat into "pure" abstraction. First, "pure" abstraction is a fiction; subjectivity is always present. Denying the subjectivity of abstraction is a way of hiding. As discussed elsewhere this book, working in abstraction and ambiguity is a privilege that white choreographers have historically enjoyed. Whereas audiences often read the work of a choreographer of color as being about their racial identity, regardless of the artist's intentions, white choreographers have the luxury of being able to choose to work in abstraction—to take their subjectivity out of their work.[275] How can white abstraction acknowledge its own whiteness?

I want to imagine a choreographic space where good form and political commitments uplift each other, rather than cancel each other out. A space that does not use politics to avoid movement research. A space that does not erase difference through abstraction. A space where the dancing can be both abstract and identity-driven. In the words of Michèle Steinwald:

> We've had such a narrow vision. That is what the binary does. Once you undo binaries in your thinking, there is never a right or a wrong, a good or a bad. Once you undo those binaries, you see more possibilities. It's not either a big improvisational process where clothes come off in ecstasy by the end of the performance or a work that is dry, linear, calculated and directive. There's so much more.[276]

Let's imagine a space where artistic excellence and politics are not mutually exclusive. Let's expect that repairing inequities is a necessary part of artistic vision.

DECOLONIZED RIGOR

Embracing a categorical messiness between activist and aesthetic values doesn't mean we ditch specificity. I want to distinguish specificity, which has value, from perfectionism, which functions as a control mechanism.[277] What does decolonized choreographic rigor look like?[278]

For me, another way into this inquiry is asking: How does my whiteness inform my ideas about choreographic specificity? Author Jess Row describes white literary craft as "an aesthetic of risk management" in which white authors, through censoring themselves and editing people of color out of their imaginations, present a controlled version of themselves and the world.[279] Row describes white literary craft as "a series of silences, defensive postures, lacunae, conscious and unconscious limitations."[280] Row argues that white authors have turned toward formal symmetries and away from "inconvenient details, glaring absences, or obvious contradictions."[281] Row argues that literary notions of craft are bound up in a tradition of white authors excising the "fat" in their work—"cutting away the parts of the story body" that authors are ashamed of, the parts they want "no one to see."[282] An extreme literary version of this, Row suggests, is the work of Gertrude Stein, where words become unmoored from meaning and the writing becomes "pure" syntax, "an obsessively detailed codex of a private, static universe."[283] White authors, Row argues, engage in the "symbolic violence" of editing the self and the world so that they can feel a sense of "imaginative autonomy."[284] Historically, in much of the white literary pantheon, there is a sense that turning away from the world is necessary in order to locate the self.

I want to apply Row's analysis of the white literary tradition to my choreographic lineage of ballet and postmodernism. These historically white-dominated dance lineages are deeply marked by forms of symbolic violence against the body (i.e., technique) and by strict temporal and spatial constraints. As a young dancer, after training in classical ballet, I trained with and performed for many white choreographers who would likely call their work "pure syntax": Merce Cunningham, Lucinda Childs, and Trisha Brown, among others. I spent the duration of my dance career in these white-dominated spaces honing my ability to execute precise form, space, and timing. I experienced this focus on form as a sanctuary for myself. To put it another way, I was allowed to hide in these spaces. The work made demands on my body and my attention, but for the most part, it left my emotional life alone. Facial expressions were unacceptable as overly theatrical. The work did not ask me to emote, to take a stand, or to be emotionally intimate with other dancers. Like all performers of concert dance, I could relate to the audience at a distance. And the audience was in the dark.

Occasionally, certain people challenged me to show up emotionally inside the abstraction. While I was dancing for Lucinda Childs, our rehearsal director challenged me to "show up as an artist, not just as an athlete." She didn't elaborate, but her comment stayed with me. Once, when I was performing a solo of Trisha Brown's called "Rage," Trisha was in the audience. After the show, I was mortified because I knew the solo had fallen flat. Backstage, she agreed. She told me to channel my own rage into the dance. This was an obvious prompt, but in the process of learning the solo, despite the title of the dance, I had not spent any time on its emotional life. I had focused only on mechanics. This was as much my failure as anyone's, but the culture of the work did not encourage me to connect my inner life to the execution of movement. The next night, I tapped into a place of ancient rage inside of me. "You nailed it," Trisha said to me after the show.

My professional dance career is now over. As a choreographer with a legacy of white abstraction in my body, I am learning how to invite my emotional life into the studio, as well as the emotional lives of the dancers who work with me.

Inviting emotional life into craft means asking: What might it look like to develop a sense of craft based in permission, not restraint? For a long time, I've felt that the only way I can make form is by unmaking it. In choreography, we all know the phrase "kill your darlings"—the accepted wisdom that you must remove beloved material for the sake of craft. In the past, I have taken this approach to an extreme by relying heavily on deconstruction as a choreographic tool—editing that isolates a small unit of movement, puts it in a different context, and/or manipulates it to get at a strangeness. I have found that these acts of alienation can lead to freedom from familiar forms. I have found that deconstruction pushes against my lineage of white formalism and in doing so, makes space for a voice that feels like my own. In the words of photographer Diane Arbus, "It's what I've never seen before that I recognize."[285]

But interrogating whiteness makes me interested in making dances with tools other than symbolic violence. Can I find my voice through tools other than refusal? Can I engage in abstraction without rejecting context? Can I make dances without closing myself off from myself?

Racial justice work and artmaking both invite us to show up emotionally. If colonized rigor turns away from the world, decolonized rigor insists on a searching dialogue between subject matter and form. I mean form on both the micro-level of the body—movement vocabulary—and the macro level of the stage—composition in time and space. Only by investigating subject matter through form will the dance's power reside in the dance itself, rather than in borrowed heat from its subject matter. In this way, form can be as important as content in socially engaged dance.

Writer Chris Kraus says, "people say my work is so personal, but the form is everything. The form is really how I arrive at how I'm going to write."[286] Similarly, poet Adrienne Rich writes:

> What are your poems about?, a stranger will sometimes ask. I don't say, "About finding form," since that would imply that form is my only concern. But without intuition and mutation, in each poem yet again, of what its form will be, I have no poem, no subject, no meaning.[287]

Writer Zadie Smith says that "everyone is born with a subject, but it is fully expressed only through a commitment to form."[288] Smith quotes the African American painter Lynette Yiadom-Boakye, talking about her artistic process:

> Over time I realised I needed to think less about the subject and more about the painting. So I began to think very seriously about colour, light, and composition. The more I worked, the more I came to realise that *the power was in the painting itself*.[289]

Form is more than a vehicle for content. Form is also something that, "like the body, possesses an intelligence of its own."[290] The power of socially engaged dance must live in the dance itself, not on its surface in the form of projection or voiceover. To get there, we must probe, burn, and strip the dance *as form*, as a way of engaging with the dance *both* as a unique language and as politics.[291]

I'm done with hiding in politics and I'm done with hiding in abstraction. In both realms, I must be willing to share my inner life. If I'm going to make a dance, the stakes must be high. I must reckon with my aesthetics and summon my poetic nerve. I must locate my body in the world, commit to a dialogic process, search for an ethical abstraction, and pursue decolonized rigor. I must feel like I need to say something through the dance that cannot be said in any other way—not through words or lawyering or protest. Otherwise, why bother?

VALUING PAUSE

A final aspect of my white dancing lineage that I want to challenge is positioning dance as an ambitious mode of will-driven production. I remember rehearsing with a choreographer in midtown New York City just two days after 9/11. Smoke, fumes, grief, and anxiety drenched the air. Pushing ahead with rehearsal in the middle of so much loss felt odd. And yet it also felt normal. I was used to ignoring my own emotional life in order to dance. Part of being a professional dancer is squeezing pleasure—ostensibly the reason we all got into dance in the first place—into the demands of training and production schedules. The show must go on.

But as I write this book, amidst the coronavirus, the show *has* stopped. Theaters and studios have been closed for months. Ensembles cannot gather. How do our bodies respond to this enforced pause? The engine of production tugs at the leash. I need a show on the calendar. I insist on rehearsing outside. I focus on projects that might manifest in two years. I keep making as a way of coping. When I do stop, I notice my exhaustion. I notice that I want to be still. When I come back to movement, I want to move in a way that simply feels good.

Part of summoning poetic nerve is making space for pause. In that space, what if we allow pleasure to dictate the choreographic process? To paraphrase my friend, poet Maxe Crandall: How can the body, and not transaction, be an occasion for dance? Even here in this book, I left pleasure until the end. How I would like pleasure to be more than an afterthought.

Part of dismantling white cultural power is examining how habits of will-driven production deny that the world is on fire. Ambition closes off feeling and curiosity. How can I build bridges between the world on fire and what comes out of me as an artist? Part of dismantling white supremacy is chipping away at the walls inside of us.

Conclusion

I'm writing the conclusion to this book amidst the coronavirus crisis, the global movement for racial justice in the wake of the police murder of George Floyd, unprecedented wildfires in the West, and a tilting of democracy into authoritarianism. 2020 magnified inequities throughout society, including in the arts. People of color continue to die from the coronavirus at far higher rates than whites.[292] Artists and arts organizations operating on the margins are suffering more than well-resourced artists, many of whom are white, and well-resourced arts organizations, many of which are white-led. The pandemic and civil unrest threaten to reify logics of scarcity as artists and arts organizations hunker down in survival mode.

I hope the arts don't go back to "normal" after this crisis is over. Normal hasn't worked. How can we open out to each other instead of close down? What are we willing to risk in order to move our communities toward justice?

Closure is incompatible with the ongoing work of cultural equity, so I won't end with any pat conclusions. What does it mean to have a radical body? The work of answering that question, and the other questions in this book, will never be over. I don't know where this line of thinking will lead. I want to believe that the dance field will continue to expand to accommodate activist visions and that in turn, new forms of dance will emerge in that expanded field. For decades, people in dance have been asking, "What's next after Judson?" Judson democratized the body; it's time to democratize the field.

Our end point is less important than our practice. Together, let's practice enduring "the weight of the unknown, the untracked, the unrealized."[293] Let's practice saying yes to hard conversations that stay unresolved. Let's practice decentering ourselves while staying engaged and accountable. Let's practice destabilizing white supremacy culture in our organizations and in the studio. Let's practice gratitude, not shame, as an engine for our work in the world. Let's make space to vision the future together, not just react to crisis.

Dance can be liberated and liberating through committed and thoughtful practice. Dance might also be liberatory by demonstrating the kind of thorough application of ethics that might make all of us better citizens. I want our movements, both bodily and collective, to pulse with compassionate engagement and courage.

I'm not an artist or an activist; I'm both. Curating as a form of community organizing is not a substitute for traditional political actions such as protesting and voting. It supplements political action with embodied imagination. This work can look like people sitting in a circle talking and listening. It can look like ritual. It can look like a room full of people moving in ways that are impossible to name. It can look like dancing.

Grounding Politics in the Body
Prompts for Studio Practice

Being in our bodies can help us shift cultural power. When I witness injustice, I feel an immediate physical reaction. Dance and sensation take us beyond language. Embracing unnameable, embodied experience is good practice for the ambiguities and uncertainties of a shifting, precarious world. Going back and forth between studio practice and curating is an invitation to connect embodied experience with critical thinking. The following prompts are designed to bring the socially engaged work of shifting cultural power into your body. Use them as points of departure for developing your own practices of embodied inquiry. Use them to anchor your work in your own physical truths. Use them to find your poetic nerve.

LANDING IN YOUR OWN BODY

Imagine an ideal space for you to arrive in your body alone. Are you in a studio or outdoors? What is the space around you like? Imagine the light, the temperature, the floor, the sounds. What forms of nourishment are available? What makes it feel safe and generative for you as an artist, in all of your identities?

What comes up for you emotionally in conjuring this vision? Longing, fear, anxiety? The idea that there is not enough money or time to make it possible? Think about someone who might help you manifest your vision of your ideal creative space. How can you ask for what you need in order to make this vision a reality? Perhaps there is a colleague, collaborator, mentor, or group you can invite to share creative space with you or realize this vision. If it is hard to give yourself this kind of time, scheduling it with other people can help you show up for your own embodied practice.

If you are working in the studio alone, how do you welcome and arrive inside your own body? You may have one way of working in your body, or you may have many. Make a list of all of the different body practices you already have, want to explore, or want to develop. This may include running, somatics, improvisation, yoga, weight training, social dance, club dancing, ballet, cycling, folk dance, classical dance, ritual, and healing practices. What you make as an artist can come from any part of you. No form of movement training is better than others. All may have something to offer. If you are deeply anchored in a specific movement practice, play with your relationship to it. Hold it tightly and hold it loosely. Do you do it as often as you would like? Do you want to explore warming up through different movement practices and traditions? Perhaps there are movement practices that are a part of your past that you would like to reclaim on new terms. Perhaps there are movement practices that you would like to let go. Reckon with and re-imagine your physical practice.

Notice how the way you prepare your body to move influences what you make as an artist. Notice if there are parts of yourself that feel left out of your studio practice. As a moving body, how can you welcome all of yourself into the work?

MOVING IN COMMUNITY

Play with different ways of preparing to move with other people. What do you prefer—moving through shared practices or everyone warming up in their own way? If you are preparing to create as a group, is it important to you or anyone else that there be a set of articulated, shared movement values in the room? If so, how are these values communicated? As a creative process unfolds, notice if certain values are absent in the work. How can warming up as a group open the door to what you want to see present in the art?

What do you need as a mover and a participant in the group in terms of ground rules for communication and boundaries? Make time in the process for people to share their personal access needs and needs about ground rules for moving together and sharing space.

How does the group acknowledge difference in training, ability, age, language preference, learning style, and body type? What are some ways in which you can create space for multiple abilities and identities in the context of a group warm-up?

In a group movement practice, who holds the power in the room? How is power and authorship shared or held? Try different models of leadership and authorship, such as single authorship, rotating authorship, and co-authorship. Notice how you contribute and what your default habits are in collaboration. Try something new. Don't surrender your voice. Don't monopolize the space.

In a solo or group movement practice, how much of the practice is improvisation? How much involves the creation and transmission of set form? How much time is spent in unknown territory? On research and question-driven exploration through the body? How much time do you want to spend in these different modes? Which modes are your favorites? Identify and give voice to your longings and curiosities as a mover among other movers.

If you are white, practice decentering yourself in conversation with other people. Try this practice in a verbal conversation as well as in a movement conversation or a movement-based creative process. In a group of people brainstorming, collaborating, or problem-solving, decenter yourself. What is difficult about this decentering? What are the benefits? What comes up for you personally? When do you need to assert your position? Around what issues? Do you use decentering as a way of hiding or avoiding engagement? How can you stay fully present, accountable, and engaged as an artist, but not in control over outcome?

If you are usually the one making decisions, what are some concrete ways in which you can give up power? If you are usually the one following someone else's lead, how can you step up and assert more power in the room? What emotions surface when you imagine taking on a different role?

How can shifting power relations open up space for new models of relationship, communication, and process, rather than simply a shift in personnel?

RECOGNIZING PRIVILEGE AND POWER IN THE STUDIO

Take time to reflect on how your privilege impacts what happens in the studio. How are you more or less vulnerable than your collaborators and colleagues? Is everyone in the room paid the same? Who in the room owns their own home? Who has multiple roommates? Who had to commute the longest to be in rehearsal? Who has family stress or medical challenges? Who is a citizen? Who has student loans?

If you are less vulnerable than others, how does this make you more resilient in the face of stress and pressure in the studio? How can you be an advocate for those who are more vulnerable than you in the creative process? If you are less vulnerable than others in the room, how can you embrace opportunities for vulnerability? Make meaningful time and space for people to check in. If you are in a position of authority, check in with other people in a meaningful way. How can you share your vulnerability without framing yourself as a victim?

Take time at the beginning of a project or contract to collectively agree on group agreements for the creative process. Ask every artist in the room about their needs, intentions, and interests. How can these opening agreements, needs, intentions, and interests hold and align the process as it unfolds?

Once movement practice begins, how does everyone participate? Inevitably, some people assert their voices more than others. If you are facilitating the process, how can you make space for everyone to show up? How can you show up as a leader without silencing others?

If you are a choreographer or lead artist who devises material or directs other people to devise, how can you generate and share material alongside others, rather than simply asking others to generate and share? Observe how your personality and other personalities show up in the room. What can you do to make the space welcoming, safe, and generative for everyone?

BEING IN AN UNCOMFORTABLE BODY

Comfort and discomfort mean something different to everyone. There is emotional discomfort and there is physical discomfort. Some dancers spend years being uncomfortable dancing for other people on other people's terms. I am interested in a different kind of discomfort. Not the kind that feels unsafe, but the kind that feels creatively interesting to you as an artist. On your own terms and in an environment where you feel safe, explore the edges of your comfort zone as a mover. What does an uncomfortable, unstable, or unfamiliar dance look like? Feel like? What would make you uncomfortable as a mover?

What would be disorienting for you as a mover? Play with light conditions, sound, velocity, contact, costumes, whether or not your first language is spoken around you.

Practice moving in uncomfortable or seemingly impossible conditions.
Be inside of your uncomfortable dance for longer than you would prefer.
Ask someone to witness and write about your uncomfortable dance.
Switch roles.
What does discomfort bring up for you emotionally?
What do you learn from your uncomfortable dance?
Write about the experience.

NAVIGATING THROUGH HYBRID FORMS

Select or create four different modes of performance address. These could include academic lecture, concert dance, improvisation, drag show, ceremony, cabaret, cypher, mime, reality TV, sketch comedy, task, ritual, etc. Include some modes of address that you feel at home in and some that feel unfamiliar, challenging, or counterintuitive. Make or borrow some material for each mode. Recognize the sources of temporarily borrowed material.

Once you have cultivated new perspectives, play with moving among these modes, like surfing different channels. Make a duet with someone else where you are each channel surfing and also in conversation. Honor these variations.

RECLAIMING YOUR RELATIONSHIP TO TIME

What if you made your studio time a sanctuary for reclaiming your relationship to time?

Tune and play with different forms of listening.

Listen to your external environment and respond with your body.

Breathe in the stillness.

Practice a long pause.

Listen to your internal landscape of sensation and respond with your body.

Be in the stillness.

Practice a long pause.

Listen to metered, regimented, and metronomic time and respond with your body.

Listen in the stillness.

Practice a long pause.

Create and listen to rhythmic pattern. Conjure rhythms that you associate with your culture, your family, your body, machines, patterns of speech, or the natural world.

Notice in the stillness.

Practice a long pause.

Listen to your weight falling through space.

Move in extreme speed and extreme slowness.

Cultivate different types of speed and different types of slowness.

Allow these and other forms of listening to take over the engine of your dancing.

Play with navigating among them.

Notice what modes you are drawn to and which you resist.

How can some modes of listening take you "out of time"?

How quickly do you work compared to other people you work with?

Do other people in the room like to move at a different pace than you?

Check in with your collaborators about pacing and how the group relates to time.

Try to avoid making anything.

What does it mean in your studio practice to move at the speed of relationship, not production?

DECOLONIZING TRANSMISSION

In the studio, make some movement or performance material with someone else or with other people.

Where is the material coming from?

Who is teaching it?

How is material transmitted—body to body? From video? Through language? In the transmission process, how and when do you express your needs and questions about the material? How much freedom do you feel to interpret the material? How obligated do you feel to mimic the teacher as exactly as possible? Is there space in the room to talk about dancer agency?

What role do you default to as a mover and collaborator?

Are you happy with the relationships in the room? If not, why not? What do you need? What does the work need? Are those two needs in tension? Who owns the movement once it exists in the space? Is there a sense that there is an "original" or truest version? Can you play with material as collective content so that everyone in the room can transform it?

If material is collectively authored, are you happy with the resulting dance from an aesthetic standpoint? If not, why not?

WORKING ON AND OFF MESSAGE

In the studio, make some movement or performance material about a specific social justice issue. In the same studio session, make some movement or performance material simply for the sake of making something without knowing what it is about. Listen to your materials: the movement phrases, the sensation of your body moving. Doodle with your body. Improvise. Follow your curiosity and follow seemingly stupid tangents.

Reflect on and compare the experience of making these two pools of material. How were the two processes different? What came up for you during each process? Cross-pollinate some of the material and methods you used in each of the above processes.

What emerges in the material? What comes up for you as a maker? How do politics show up in the body and in the material? What elements in the work hold the political content? How does the dancing itself "read to other people?" How obvious or explicit do you need the work's message to be?

PRACTICING REFUSAL

As an artist, who do you make your work for? What is your relationship to audience? What is your relationship to the dominant culture's gaze? In what ways have you internalized the expectations of dominant society? What external forces influence your definition of a "successful" dance? Make something that refuses to satisfy any of these qualities.

Develop an improvisational score exploring ideas of visibility and invisibility. How can you place yourself in space and in relationship to the architecture to make yourself more visible? Less visible? Feel free to collect and use props (furniture, clothing). Try the same prompt, but working with a partner. How can you use each other to make yourself more or less visible?

Play with moving without arriving in a nameable shape or state. Then play with moving in very clear, defined ways, in terms of both shape and quality. Travel back and forth between legibility and illegibility. What is it like to transition between the two?

STAYING IN OUR BODIES AMIDST CONFLICT: WORKING WITH EMBODIED HABITS OF DISENGAGEMENT[294]

When you are faced with stress or conflict, what are your habits of self-protection? Read this list of defensive postures and see which resonate with you:

- Denial/avoidance
- Defensiveness
- Perfectionism
- Rationality/intellectualizing
- Self-absorption
- Silence/withdrawal
- Blaming others
- Numbness
- Urgency/franticness

How do you know when you are in one of your default defensive habits?

What does the defensive habit feel like in your body? What does it sound like in your thoughts?

What does it look like in your posture, movement, and actions? How has this defensive habit helped you in the past?

How has this defensive habit not served you?

If you didn't use this defensive habit, what might you need to feel instead? When you notice yourself in your defensive habit, what might help you return to fuller engagement with others?

CONNECTING TO JOY AND RESILIENCE

Why do you dance? Sometimes as professional dancers we lose connection to the reason we started dancing in the first place. What can you do today to reconnect with the joy and pleasure of dancing? Maybe it means taking a class for fun instead of training. Maybe it means having a dance party in your kitchen.

Making art and being politically engaged can be exhausting. Make time to take care of yourself. Take some time to forget about your art as a career. Reconnect with your passions and your desires. Why do you make art? What feeds your spirit? Do what nourishes and recharges you. If you feel burned out, take a break. That could mean being with other artists. It could mean being with other people who aren't artists. It could mean being alone or with a pet. Go for a hike. Go to the beach or the park. Read some poetry. Make a pot of delicious tea. Call a friend who makes you laugh.

QUESTIONING THE ASSUMPTIONS BEHIND STUDIO PRACTICE

What assumptions do we carry into the studio? Read through the below list and see if any apply to your practice. I associate these assumptions with what I will call "colonized" choreography.[295] I write this embedded in a web of conversations and relationships with dancers and choreographers who are actively working on ways to liberate their work; this writing is indebted to these relationships.[296]

TWENTY ASSUMPTIONS BEHIND COLONIZED CHOREOGRAPHY (ONE OR SOME OR ALL MAY APPLY)

1. Conditions must be perfect in order for me to create. This might mean: I must have solitude or I must have certain people in the

room. No mirrors or mirrors. No sound or the perfect sound. A bare studio. No distractions like emotions, discomfort, or world events.

2. The dance must be clean. This might mean clean transitions, invisible effort, and no falling unless it is the performance of a fall.

3. There is an original, truest, singular version of all movement material. This original source lives in one person's body (or in a video of that person's body). Questions about movement are resolved by going to this singular source.

4. The dance must be beautiful.

5. The dancers fit a particular definition of physical beauty, ability, and training.

6. If politics are present, they must be sanitized and aesthetically pleasing.

7. Content must translate into pattern.

8. Formal symmetry is good.

9. The rules of making the dance are fixed. These rules cannot be upset, challenged, or changed. The terms of the creative process are obscure, unspoken, or run on autopilot.

10. The form of the dance does not question itself. There are no competing forms, languages, or modes of performance threatening the authority or stability of the world of the dance.

11. The artist is not transparent with the financial terms of the creative process: artist payment, funding sources, project budget.

12. The space is white-dominated. People of color are absent or present only as tokens.

13. The choreographer's ideas must be protected. The choreographer's ideas trump other ideas. No one in the room feels empowered to tell the choreographer that they have a bad idea.

14. The choreographer's initial or gut instincts are always right.

15. The choreographer's self provides the basis for compositional systems.

16. The dance is legible.

17. The dance is visible.

18. The dance is not too long.

19. The dance is entertaining.

20. The dance is a hermetically sealed space.

TWENTY-FIVE PRACTICES FOR DECOLONIZING DANCE (AND FINDING YOUR POETIC NERVE)

How can you liberate your movement and creative practices? How can you anchor your art practices in authentic community and in trust? Write a list. When you begin a project, co-create a list with your artistic collaborators. Below are some possibilities. Pick some to try. If I were to implement all of the below prompts, I might not end up making a dance at all. But I want to put myself in that space, invite others to be in the space with me, and listen for what comes next.

Practices of decolonization are also tools for locating your poetic nerve. Poetic nerve does not mean surrendering authorship. It does not mean emotional retreat or disengagement. It means going beyond yourself, and then back within again, and then again out past yourself, and so on, in a constant conversation between the dance and the world.

1. Collaborate with people and places that destabilize and challenge authorship.
2. Practice sustained listening.
3. Encourage imperfection and doubt (yours and others).
4. Slow down. Value pause. Waste time. Wander.
5. Value pleasure.
6. Invite excess, kitsch, camp, sentimentality, and overmuchness.
7. Orient the dance and its systems outward. Make in relationship. Make dance in the mess of the world.
8. Allow the dancing to be invisible, ambiguous, and illegible.
9. There is no original, truest version of movement. Movement material is collectively owned and authored.
10. Allow edges to be a part of the landscape of the dance. Refuse a fixed front.
11. Be transparent about your needs and your fallibility as an artist. Be clear about the terms of the work with yourself and your collaborators. Name collaborative periods of work; name when you need to author or edit.
12. Acknowledge and credit sources of movement, both in the studio ("This is a phrase that Jane made." "I pulled this idea off of YouTube.") and in promotional materials ("This dance was co-created by…").

13. Allow for multiplicity: multiple voices, multiple variables, multiple vocabularies. Develop a vocabulary of inclusion sourced from multiple bodies. What does it mean to assert authorship amidst multiplicity?

14. Acknowledge and pay attention to how everyone in the room works at different processing speeds. Orient the process to different people's sense of time.

15. Explore what it might mean for the dance to be porous. What can you let into the space of the dance?

16. Practice making without a show in mind. Hold the creative process more lightly while still staying engaged, accountable, and supportive of others in the space.

17. Allow improvisation to take over the process.

18. Allow for sustained movement research outside of the task of making. Find creative modes beyond composition and mimicry.

19. The space should not be white-dominated. People of color should be fully integrated, engaged, empowered, acknowledged, and respected in the cast, crew, and artistic staff.

20. Question your choices. Question instinctual preferences. Work with a palette you despise. Stay with an idea much longer than you think is appropriate.

21. Invite other people's emotional lives into the work.

22. Invite other people to hijack the process.

23. Practice financial transparency about artist pay, project budget, and funding sources.

24. Show up with no agenda. Work with what and who is in the room.

25. Be vulnerable.

The Bridge Project 2010–2020
An Annotated Archive

Below is an annotated archive of The Bridge Project's history over the last ten years, with commentary about my motivations and learning curve. I created the titles that follow each year or collection of years in hindsight and for the purpose of this archive. Many of these programs are discussed in more detail in this book as case studies.

2010–2013: EARLY YEARS/THE SHARED PROGRAM MODEL

Yvonne Rainer ((New York City/*Trio A*), Molissa Fenley/New York City) (*Mass Balance*), and Hope Mohr (Bay Area/*Far from Perfect*)
Theater Artaud, San Francisco
March 4–6, 2010

Liz Gerring (New York City/*She Dreams in Code*) and Hope Mohr (Bay Area/ *The Unsayable*)
Z Space, San Francisco
March 3–6, 2011

Dušan Týnek (New York City/*Transparent Walls* and *Base Pairs*) and Hope Mohr (Bay Area/*Reluctant Light*)
Z Space, San Francisco
March 22–24, 2012

Susan Rethorst (Philadelphia/*Behold Bold Sam Dog*) and Hope Mohr (Bay Area/*Failure of the Sign is the Sign*)
ODC Theater, San Francisco
May 2–5, 2013

UNDERVIEW

In 2010, I had recently relocated to the Bay Area from New York, where I performed with many postmodern choreographers, all of whom were white and in the Judson Dance Theater lineage. I began curating colleagues and idols from that circle. I was eager to place my own work in conversation with them as a way of testing and learning about my own choreographic voice.

The Bridge Project began in 2010 featuring *Trio A*, arguably the most important work to come out of the Judson Dance Theater pantheon. Choreographer Pat Catterson, whom I danced for in New York, set the work on me and dancer Robbie Cook. I wanted to pair the work with other voices, so I invited choreographer Molissa Fenley to perform her solo *Mass Balance*. Fenley was at that time a mentor of mine through Choreographers in Mentorship Exchange (CHIME), a program of the Margaret Jenkins Dance Company. Also on the program was a new work of my own, *Far from Perfect*.

For the next three years, I continued to invite choreographers I had close relationships with to share programs, including Liz Gerring (2011), whom I danced for in New York, and Dušan Týnek (2012), with whom I danced for Lucinda Childs. In 2013, wanting to facilitate an exchange with bigger impact, I invited Philadelphia-based choreographer Susan Rethorst to set her *Behold Bold Sam Dog* on a multiracial group of seven female choreographers from the Bay Area: Katie Faulkner, Christy Funsch, Aura Fischbeck, Erin Mei-Ling Stuart, Deborah Karp, Phoenicia Pettyjohn, Peiling Kao, and me. This allowed local choreographers to benefit from an exchange with an influential, elder choreographer from outside the region.

The shared program model was an easy way to start curating. But as I would come to realize, tethering programs to my voice and ego sacrificed a more generous invitation to a broader public. Over the past ten years, the more I have decentered myself from public programs, the more successful these programs have become in terms of facilitating exchange and benefitting other artists. As this book discusses, decentering the curator is especially essential when the curator is white, like me.

2014: LOOKING AT LINEAGE THROUGH THE FEMALE BODY
HAVE WE COME A LONG WAY, BABY?

Featuring:
Anna Halprin (Bay Area/*The Courtesan and the Crone*)
Simone Forti (Los Angeles/*News Animations*)
Hope Mohr (Bay Area/performing *Carnation*, Lucinda Childs' 1964 solo)
Peiling Kao (Bay Area/ performing *s(oft is)hard*, a solo by Hope Mohr)

Program included, in addition to performances, a panel discussion with Anna Halprin, Simone Forti, and Hope Mohr, moderated by Stanford University dance historian Dr. Janice Ross. Produced in association with the Joe Goode Annex, San Francisco, September 26–27, 2014.

UNDERVIEW

Have We Come A Long Way, Baby? came directly from my interest in curating through a feminist lens. Also, as a Bay Area native who danced for several members of the Judson Dance Theater (Lucinda Childs, Trisha Brown, and Douglas Dunn), I felt that the New York-centric hullabaloo about the fiftieth anniversary of Judson had sorely neglected the influence of Anna Halprin.[297] I wanted to curate an intergenerational program that celebrated the wisdom of the female body. Anna Halprin (born 1920), Simone Forti (born 1935), Lucinda Childs (born 1940), myself (born 1971), and Peiling Kao (born 1973) shared the evening. The solo that Halprin performed, *The Courtesan and the Crone*, explicitly addresses the aging body in motion. Many lines of influence ran through the program. Forti studied with Halprin before joining the Judson Dance Theater in New York. Childs was a part of Judson; I danced for Childs. Kao and I have collaborated for many years; our lineage is more lateral than linear, and thus for me our relationship signified a more contemporary way of thinking about dance legacy.

2015: CENTERING CRITICAL THINKING
REWRITING DANCE

Featuring:
Jeanine Durning (New York City/*inging* (performance) and *what we do when we do the thing we do before we know what we are doing* (workshop))
Deborah Hay (Austin), Alva Noë (Bay Area), Michèle Steinwald (Minneapolis) (*Reorganizing Ourselves*)

Gerald Casel, Maurya Kerr, Hope Mohr, Megan Nicely, Lauren Simpson/Jenny Stulberg, and Maureen Whiting (Bay Area/*Talk the Walk: Local Artists at the Intersection of Language and Choreographic Thinking*)

Program included, in addition to performances, a Conversation with Hope Mohr & Jeanine Durning and Screening of Deborah Hay's *"O,O"* at the Center for New Music in San Francisco. Co-produced with Counterpulse at the Joe Goode Annex, San Francisco, November 4–6, 2015.

UNDERVIEW

I was still interested in the Judson lineage and so approached Deborah Hay. I was also a fan of Jeanine Durning, a longtime collaborator of Hay's. Putting the two together on a program made sense not only from a lineage perspective, but also because both artists work at the intersection of language and dance. Durning's *inging* featured the practice of unscripted, nonstop language as performance. *Reorganizing Ourselves* was a performative lecture featuring choreographer Hay and philosopher and cognitive scientist Alva Noë discussing perception, consciousness, and the links between art and science. *Reorganizing Ourselves* concluded with a salon-style discussion with audience members facilitated by curator Michèle Steinwald. The critical thinking and hybrid form present in *Rewriting Dance* set the stage for later iterations of The Bridge Project that would commission hybrid work. Finally, it was becoming clear to me that in order to generate wide-reaching exchange in the community, I needed to provide performance opportunities for local artists alongside artists from beyond the Bay Area. I invited six local choreographers to perform as part of the program alongside my work. This was the last year that my own choreography appeared as part of The Bridge Project.

2016: FRAMING LINEAGE IN AN EXPANDED FIELD
TEN ARTISTS RESPOND TO "LOCUS"

Featuring
   Commissioned Artists (all artists were based in the Bay Area):
   Xandra Ibarra (*a view from outside the cube*)
   Affinity Project (*Color grid with talking (after Locus)*)
   Cheryl Leonard (*Asterisms*)
   Amy Foote (*Never mind the notes you missed*)
   Peiling Kao (*per[mute]ing*)
   Gregory Dawson (*15*)

Larry Arrington (*quarter*)
Gerald Casel (*Taglish*)
Tracy Taylor Grubbs (*per[mute]ing* and *Color grid with talking (after Locus)*)
Frances Richard (*Locus poem*)

Repertory Dancers (performing *Locus Solo* (1975) at the start of the program and during intermission):
Sarah Chenoweth
Hope Mohr
Jenny Stulberg
Karla Quintero

Lead Teaching Artist and Rehearsal Director/Stager of *Locus Solo*: Diane Madden, Co-Artistic Director, Trisha Brown Dance Company

Program included, in addition to performances, an audition workshop for dancers, a two-week residency for commissioned artists, open rehearsals, a free public talk about the works of Trisha Brown by Diane Madden, and post-show discussions with the commissioned artists. Presented in association with Yerba Buena Center for the Arts, September 10–October 15, 2016.

UNDERVIEW

As a former Trisha Brown dancer, I wanted to facilitate a program that brought Brown's work to the Bay Area. But after *Have We Come a Long Way, Baby?*, I was hungry to explore lineage in an expanded field—to commission artists from a range of artistic disciplines and cultural backgrounds to engage with dance legacy. I wanted the focus to be on facilitating the authorship of new work, rather than re-staging repertory. However, I still wanted repertory on the program to provide historical context.

Ten Artists Respond to "Locus" was a multidisciplinary engagement with the work of choreographer Trisha Brown that commissioned ten Bay Area artists from multiple disciplines to learn Brown's dance *Locus* (1975) and respond with new works. The project culminated in ten commissioned premieres, all in one evening, alongside performances of *Locus Solo* (a version of the original *Locus* quartet) by four different Bay Area dancers.

Rather than select the commissioned artists myself, I paid several established artists in fields other than modern dance to each nominate an artist for a commission. This community curatorial council included the performing arts program staff of YBCA (at that time, Marc Bamuthi Joseph, Isabel Yri-goyen, and Claire Shoun) who coproduced the program; choreographer Dohee Lee; composer Adam Fong; composer Pamela Z; theater director Erika Chong Shuch; and performance artist Keith Hennessy. This curatorial council acti-vated a wider swath of the art community than if I alone had made the com-missioning decisions. I did not include myself as one of the commissioned artists, but I was one of the dancers who performed *Locus Solo* on the program.

The *Locus* project was the first time that the Trisha Brown Dance Company had allowed one of Brown's dances to be transmitted beyond the company for the explicit purpose of inspiring new works of art by artists who hailed from disciplines other than dance. The ten selected artists participated in an inten-sive two-week workshop with Diane Madden, Co-Artistic Director of the Trisha Brown Dance Company, which included daily morning movement classes and afternoon sessions dedicated to learning *Locus*.

The *Locus* program showed me the importance of making space for iden-tity in the context of considering the dance canon. I would apply these lessons three years later when The Bridge Project produced a similarly-structured program engaging with the legacy of Merce Cunningham.

In 2016, in order to support the *Locus* project, HMD secured funding from the National Endowment for the Arts for the first time. This national funding was a major milestone in the growth of The Bridge Project. It encouraged me to have ambitious curatorial vision and to situate The Bridge Project in a national dance landscape. Also in 2016, after seven years of applying, HMD was added to the roster of organizations that receive general operating support from San Francisco's Grants for the Arts. This grant, our first source of general operating support, was an important step in securing HMD's financial sustainability.

2017: CENTERING CRITICAL THINKING AND GENDER JUSTICE
RADICAL MOVEMENTS: GENDER AND POLITICS IN PERFORMANCE

Featuring:
>Becca Blackwell (New York City/*They, Themself and Schmerm*)
>Judith Butler (Bay Area/*Ordinary Practices of the Radical Body*)
>Monique Jenkinson (Bay Area/*Ordinary Practices of the Radical Body*)
>Jack Halberstam (New York City/*dance of darkness: a performance, a conversation, a rehearsal for the future*)
>boychild (Los Angeles/*dance of darkness: a performance, a conversation, a rehearsal for the future*)

Lisa Evans (Bay Area/*How I Got to Femme*)
Maryam Rostami (Bay Area/*Untitled 1396*)
Julie Tolentino (Bay Area/*a.u.l.e.*)
Amara Tabor-Smith (Bay Area/*a.u.l.e.*)
Larry Arrington (Bay Area/*a.u.l.e.*)
Xandra Ibarra (Bay Area/*a.u.l.e.*)
Maurya Kerr (Bay Area/*a.u.l.e.*)
Debra Levine (New York City/*a.u.l.e.*)
Scot Nakagawa (Seattle/*a.u.l.e.*)
Julian Carter (Bay Area/*Audience Salon: What does it mean to have a radical body?*)

Program ran from September 18 to November 12, 2017 and included, in addition to performances, an Audience Reader; an audience salon that allowed the public to discuss these readings and the core question animating the festival, *What does it mean to have a radical body?*; and post-show discussions following every performance. Coproduced with CounterPulse at: Z Space Below, CounterPulse, and the Joe Goode Annex, San Francisco.

UNDERVIEW

The *Radical Movements* festival came out of my desire to commission and present hybrid performance forms that interrogated notions of gender from a variety of perspectives. While co-directing a production of Anne Carson's *Antigonick* in 2015, I learned that cast member Monique Jenkinson was a fan of gender theorist Judith Butler. I thought it would be exciting to pair Jenkinson, who performs gender as a cis-female drag queen, with Butler, who coined the idea of gender as performance. I approached both of them with the invitation to create something together for The Bridge Project. They accepted. The rest of the program flowed naturally from this pairing as I thought of other artists who were working with performance in unique ways to challenge ideas around gender. In order to build a framework of critical thinking around the program, I asked all of the participating artists to respond to the prompt: "What does it mean to have a radical body?" I had already been planning the program when Trump was elected; *Radical Movements* gained urgency against the ominous background of the new administration's sexist, homophobic, racist, xenophobic, and transphobic ideologies.

The *Radical Movements* program was the first time that I created an Audience Reader to accompany a public program.[298] I have since continued this practice with every major program of The Bridge Project. The Bridge Project's

Audience Readers compile writings and interviews about and by featured artists and the program's themes. My intentions behind the Audience Readers are to encourage critical thinking and situate programs in larger cultural conversations. Another desire behind the Audience Readers is to weave connections between the audience and the artist.

Often there is a disconnect between artist and audience. This disconnect is especially common in venues with built-in or subscription audiences who come to programs out of allegiance to a venue, not an artist. Because The Bridge Project partners with different venues, we need to build programmatic context anew with every program. This lack of readymade context presents an opportunity to set intentions around how to frame a program and how we want to engage the public. An Audience Reader provides a variety of entry points into a program and can lengthen the arc of engagement for an audience member. I have also found that the process of putting together an Audience Reader built around the participating artists helps me educate myself about the broader political, cultural, and historical context of the work. In this way, I can engage in thoughtful discussions with artists and audience.

Often for me, reading a book will directly lead to programming decisions. For example, after reading Aruna D'Souza's *Whitewalling: Art, Race, and Protest in 3 Acts,* I suggested her as a guest speaker to Gerald Casel as part of his 2018 Community Engagement Residency, *Dancing Around Race.* Casel liked the idea. We invited her, D'Souza accepted, and she was the headline speaker at the project's first public gathering.[299]

2017: BUILDING LONG-TERM RELATIONSHIPS WITH ARTISTS
2016–2017 COMMUNITY ENGAGEMENT RESIDENCY: JULIE TOLENTINO AND THE HARD CORPS

Featuring all Bay Area-based artists:
    Lead Artist Julie Tolentino
Artist Cohort: Amara Tabor-Smith, Larry Arrington, Xandra Ibarra, and
    Maurya Kerr
March 2017–March 2018

UNDERVIEW

Ever since 2016's *Ten Artists Respond to "Locus,"* I had been thinking about nonlinear approaches to dance legacy. I was curious about structures that could build lateral lineage through peer relationships. When I invited Julie Tolentino to participate in *Radical Movements*, I asked her what she wanted to do on the program. She said that she wanted to work over a long period of time with a small cohort of local artists. This desire coincided with my interest in cultivating the lateral lines of influence that sustain creative communities. In response, I created the Community Engagement Residency (CER), a program that supports artists for a full year to work in community, however they define it.

From the beginning, core values of the residency have been artist autonomy, the intersection of artmaking and activism, and the fostering of relationships among artists. These values emerged from the mutual respect and listening that marked my relationship with Julie Tolentino. This relationship established a baseline for the residency of listening, honoring, and responding to artist needs.

In its first two years (2017–2018), the residency offered $9,000 to one lead artist. In 2019, we expanded the number of lead artists to three, with each lead artist receiving $6,000. These artist fees are in addition to a space budget, production and marketing support, grant writing mentorship, fees for guest speakers and collaborators the lead artist wants to bring into the process, and a materials budget. In the first two years of the residency, HMD also paid stipends to artists whom the lead artist selected as mentees or collaborators. In 2019, when we expanded the number of lead artists, HMD began asking lead artists to be responsible for paying their artist collaborators. In 2021, HMD increased the lead artist stipend to $8,000 per lead artists per year and expanded the duration of the residency to a year and a half in order to provide more sustained support and to cultivate overlap and interaction among cohorts.

Local artists involved in the Community Engagement Residency have become increasingly interwoven into The Bridge Project not only through performing and leading public programs, but also through involvement in curatorial decisions. As the communities that The Bridge Project supports have changed, it has become increasingly urgent to change the organization itself so that our internal structures reflect the same commitment to cultural equity[300] as our public programs.

In 2017, HMD secured two new sources of funding that were instrumental in making The Bridge Project possible. First, we were awarded a three-year capacity-building "Impact Grant" from the Kenneth Rainin Foundation for general operating support. We could not use this for paying artists, but we could use it to pay staff, which amplified our programming capacity. Second, we started receiving funding from the California Arts Council in support of the Community Engagement Residency; this funding source has remained the CER's core source of financial support.

2018: LINEAGE AND RACE
PARAMODERNITIES

> Featuring:
> Netta Yerushalmy (New York City) (Concept, Choreography, and Direction/Lead Artist)

> Collaborators:
> Thomas DeFrantz (Durham, North Carolina)
> Maxe Crandall (Bay Area)
> Jos Lavery (Bay Area)
> David Kishik (New York City)
> Jennifer Brody (Bay Area)
> Claudia La Rocco (Bay Area)

Paramodernities was presented February 22-25, 2018 in association with ODC Theater with promotional support from SFMOMA's Open Space Limited Edition, an Open Space partnership with CounterPulse, The Lab, ODC Theater, Performance at SFMOMA, and Z Space, exploring questions of legacy and lineage.

UNDERVIEW

When I first saw Netta Yerushalmy doing a work-in-progress showing of her Martha Graham installation of her massive lineage project, *Paramodernities*, in New York in 2016, I knew it was a perfect fit with my curatorial interests in reframing dance history and hybrid performance forms. *Paramodernities*, conceived and directed by Yerushalmy, was an ambitious six-part series of multidisciplinary lecture-performances or dance-experiments generated through deconstructions of landmark modern choreographies, performed alongside contributions by scholars and writers who situate these iconic works and artists within the larger project of modernism. For the work's West Coast debut, Yerushalmy shared three of the project's six installments—her responses to Vaslav Nijinsky, Alvin Ailey, and Merce Cunningham—followed by public discussions. HMD partnered with Jacob's Pillow, New York Live Arts, and the National Performance Network to co-commission the work, which had its world premiere at Jacob's Pillow in August 2018, following The Bridge Project performances in San Francisco.

Paramodernities cultivated several important relationships among artists that would inform future programs of The Bridge Project. Gerald Casel, the lead artist in *Dancing Around Race* (discussed below), was a performer in the Balanchine chapter of *Paramodernitie*s; Thomas DeFrantz, the scholar and artist featured in the Alvin Ailey chapter of *Paramodernities*, would return to the Bay Area to participate in Casel's *Dancing Around Race* later that year. Through *Paramodernities*, I first met Claudia La Rocco, the writer featured in the Merce Cunningham chapter of *Paramodernities*; in 2019, she and I became co-curators of The Bridge Project exploring Cunningham's legacy, *Signals from the West: Bay Area Artists in Conversation with Merce Cunningham at 100.* Through *Paramodernities*, I also met Maxe Crandall, another writer featured in the West Coast Cunningam chapter of *Paramodernities*; Maxe became one of ten commissioned artists in *Signals from the West.* Maxe and I, separate from The Bridge Project, also went on to co-create *extreme lyric I,* a dance play inspired by Anne Carson's translations of the Greek poet Sappho, and we continue to collaborate.

2017–2018 COMMUNITY ENGAGEMENT RESIDENCY: *DANCING AROUND RACE*

Featuring all Bay Area-based artists:
Lead Artist Gerald Casel
Artist Cohort: Zulfikar Ali Bhutto, Sammay Dizon, David Herrera, Yayoi
      Kambara, Raissa Simpson
March 2017–March 2018

UNDERVIEW

For the second year of the Community Engagement Residency, HMD invited Gerald Casel to be the lead artist. Casel was one of the artists commissioned to make work in response to Trisha Brown in *Ten Artists Respond to "Locus"* in 2016. For his Community Engagement Residency, Casel did not want to make a dance. He wanted to talk with people. And so *Dancing Around Race* was a year-long series of private and public dialogues. Some were inward-facing and behind closed doors with invited guests (writers, presenters, educators, and other stakeholders in the dance scene). Some were public gatherings that invited the community into *Dancing Around Race*'s process. Each public gathering was anchored by a leading thinker from outside the region (art writer Aruna D'Souza from Boston; Barbara Bryan, Director of Movement Research in New York; and artist and scholar Thomas DeFrantz from Duke

University). In addition to funding from the California Arts Council, *Dancing Around Race* was also supported by an Organizational Project Grant from the San Francisco Arts Commission.

With *Dancing Around Race*, I entered into working relationships with many more artists of color. I also entered into a multitude of conversations about race with funders, writers, educators, and activists beyond dance. These conversations, which are ongoing, have underscored my awareness of the pressing need for me, as a white curator, to use my access and privilege to shift cultural power to artists of color.

2019: LINEAGE AND CULTURAL EQUITY
SIGNALS FROM THE WEST: BAY AREA ARTISTS IN CONVERSATION WITH MERCE CUNNINGHAM AT 100

Featuring:
Commissioned Artists (all Bay Area-based):
   Sofía Córdova (*Underwater Moonlight (days of blood and milk)*)
   Alex Escalante (*PARIS*)
   Maxe Crandall (*STOP PLAY :: QUINCUNX*) (performance)
   Dazaun Soleyn (*((Study)one)*)
   Danishta Rivero (*Tejidos/Weavings, or No puedo hablar can mi voz sino con mis voces*)
   Julie Moon (*STOP PLAY :: QUINCUNX*) (performance and installation)
   Christy Funsch (*Moves Cords Names*)
   Jenny Odell (*Merce Bau*)
   Nicole Peisl (*for_rest*)
   Sophia Wang (*Work in Place*)

Repertory Dancers (performing excerpts from *Scramble* (1967), *Roaratorio* (1983), *Change of Address* (1992), *BIPED* (1999), and *Fluid Canvas* (2002)):
   Sarah Cecilia Bukowski
   Traci Finch
   Emily Hansel
   Stacey Yuen

Inherited Bodies program:
   Snowflake Towers
   Jarrel Phillips
   Sara Shelton Mann
   Nadhi Thekkek

Lead Teaching Artists/Rehearsal Directors for Repertory: Rashaun Mitchell
and Silas Riener, former members of the Merce Cunningham Dance
Company

In addition to performances, the program included an audition workshop
for dancers, a two-week artist residency for commissioned artists, two public
salons, an artist talk among co-curators Hope Mohr and Claudia LaRocco and
lead teaching artist Rashaun Mitchell, and an Audience Reader. The *Signals
from the West* program also included an event called *Inherited Bodies*, which was
an evening of artist lecture demonstrations responding to the prompt: How do
you honor, challenge, and resist the past? Claudia La Rocco and I organized
Inherited Bodies in order to make space for dialogue and performance that
explored lineage but was not rooted in the work of Merce Cunningham. Co-produced with SFMOMA's Open Space, the Merce Cunningham Trust, and ODC
Theater at ODC Theater, August 10–November 9, 2019.

UNDERVIEW

In 2017, I received emails from Brenda Way, Artistic Director of ODC,
and from Claudia La Rocco, Editor-in-Chief of SFMOMA's Open Space, both
asking if The Bridge Project would be interested in partnering with their institutions and the Merce Cunningham Trust to co-produce an event in conjunction with the one hundredth anniversary of Merce Cunningham's birth.
HMD is a company in residence at ODC Theater. SFMOMA's Open Space is
the museum's interdisciplinary publishing and commissioning platform; for
this partnership, Open Space would commission a series of writings in relationship to the live public programs. I had a personal connection to Cunningham's work, having trained on scholarship at the Cunningham studio for over
a year as a young dancer in New York. I was thrilled about a new opportunity
to re-engage with dance lineage in an experimental way.

As with *Ten Artists Respond to "Locus"* in 2016, *Signals from the West* commissioned ten Bay Area artists to engage with the work of Merce Cunningham
and make new work in response. These new works premiered alongside performances of Cunningham repertory excerpts by four Bay Area dancers. There
were three co-curators: Julie Potter, Director of ODC Theater, La Rocco, and
I. We invited ten Bay Area artists from the visual, literary, and performing arts
to be in workshop with each other, along with choreographers and former Cunningham dancers Rashaun Mitchell and Silas Riener: an experiment for every-

one. Then we asked these ten artists to make something in dialogue with this experience, to be presented in tandem with the repertory excerpts.

As co-curators, we wanted to create a space for contemporary cultural exchange between individuals with different bodies of knowledge; to make room for debate and communion across disciplines, generations, and geographies. I wanted to apply what I had learned from *Ten Artists Respond to "Locus"* (2016) and *Dancing Around Race* (2018) by approaching choreographic transmission in an expanded field—a multidisciplinary space in which dialogue about identity occurred hand in hand with physical engagement. I also wanted to be more intentional in creating a space for artists to ask big questions about dance lineage and identity.

HMD was more successful in raising money for *Signals from the West* than with any other program in The Bridge Project's history. I attribute this fundraising success to The Bridge Project's demonstrated track record of engaging with dance legacy; the multidisciplinary premise of the project; the organizational partnerships assembled for the project, which included high-profile institutions like SFMOMA and the Merce Cunningham Trust; and Cunningham's fame. Fundraising success creates pressures to repeat similar programs. Some members of HMD's Board have encouraged me to find a way to replicate the program with another dance icon. But I'm suspicious of this logic of success as antithetical to experimentation. How can curators bring resources to dance that is not tethered to well-known institutions and famous white men?

2018–2019 COMMUNITY ENGAGEMENT RESIDENCY:
LATINXTENSIONS; AESTHETIC SHIFT: A DANCE LAB FOR EQUITABLE PRACTICES; AND QTBIPOC PERFORMING ARTIST HIVE

> Featuring Lead Artists (all Bay Area-based):
> David Herrera (*LatinXtensions*)
> Yayoi Kambara (*Aesthetic Shift: A Dance Lab for Equitable Practices*)
> Estrellx Supernova (formerly known as randy reyes) with Daria Garina
>   (*QTBIPOC Performing Artist Hive*)

UNDERVIEW

Parallel to *Signals from the West*, The Bridge Project continued to engage in long-term, equity-driven partnerships with local artists through our Community Engagement Residency. When *Dancing Around Race* came to an end, it was obvious that the work had only just begun. In the interest of building on that work, we decided in the third year of the Community Engagement Residency to support not one, but three artists. Two of these artists, David Herrera and Yayoi Kambara, were in Casel's *Dancing Around Race* cohort; Estrellx Supernova (formerly known as randy reyes), the third lead artist, attended many of the *Dancing Around Race* events. Herrera developed and led *LatinXtensions*, a culturally-specific mentorship and networking program for Latinx choreographers; Kambara developed and led *Aesthetic Shift, A Dance Lab for Equitable Practices*, a peer-to-peer studio process focused on developing physical practices that align with cultural equity values; and Estrellx Supernova invited their colleague Daria Garina to co-develop and co-lead the *QTBIPOC Performing Artist Hive*, an artist collective with rotating leadership.

My relationships with the lead artists in the Community Engagement Residency continued to illuminate the pressing need for HMD, the organization behind The Bridge Project, to evolve toward distributed leadership and increase artist ownership over programmatic decisions.

2020: POWER SHIFT
POWER SHIFT: IMPROVISATION, ACTIVISM, AND COMMUNITY

Featuring:
    Nigel Campbell (New York City)
    Sherwood Chen (Marseille/Bay Area)
    Yalini Dream (New York City)
    Daria Garina (Bay Area)
    Rosemary Hannon (Bay Area)
    Tammy Johnson (Bay Area)
    Liz Lerman (Tempe, Arizona)
    Paloma McGregor (New York City)
    Amy Miller (New York City)
    Hope Mohr (Bay Area)
    Maurice Moore (Bay Area)
    Ranu Mukherjee (Bay Area)
    Bhumi B. Patel (Bay Area)
    Jarrel Phillips (Bay Area)
    Estrellx Supernova (Bay Area)
    Beatrice Thomas (Bay Area)
    Judith Sánchez Ruíz (Berlin)
    sam wentz (Los Angeles)

This program took place September 13–November 22, 2020, outside, online, at the Joe Goode Annex, and at the Center for Empowering Refugees and Immigrants.

UNDERVIEW

In 2020, we marked the tenth anniversary of The Bridge Project with a program called *Power Shift: Activism, Improvisation, and Community.* This title refers to the potential of improvisation and activism to shift dominant cultural narratives. It also reflects internal shifts in HMD. Although in previous years I'd partnered with curators outside HMD to implement programs, before 2020 I'd never given over curatorial power inside my own organization. In 2020, this changed when HMD announced that The Bridge Project would be co-directed by HMD's two staff members, Cherie Hill and Karla Quintero, both female artists of color. This signified a major shift within HMD's internal decision-making structure. For me, this shift to a co-curatorial model felt exciting as a form of creative work itself demanding imagination and dialogue.

Power Shift focused on improvisation. This focus felt like a fitting response to navigating uncertain, precarious times, especially as we shifted the entire festival online and outdoors in response to COVID-19. Also, as HMD moved away from known territory as an organization, it felt fitting to focus on a mode of movement other than set forms.

For the first time, The Bridge Project in 2020 explicitly named decentering whiteness as part of its curatorial goals. Many people mistakenly assume that dance improvisation began in the 1960s and 70s with Judson Church and Contact Improvisation—two spaces historically dominated by white artists. *Power Shift* addressed this gap in the field by centering improvisational makers and practices from traditions beyond white postmodernism, including Latinx voices, voices from African dance, jazz aesthetics, social and street dance, and Capoeira. Twelve of the eighteen featured artists are POC.

2019–2020 COMMUNITY ENGAGEMENT RESIDENCY

Lead Artists (all Bay Area-based):
Hannah Ayasse, Chibueze Crouch, Zoe Donnellycolt (*Performance Primers*)
Jarrel Phillips (*Living Folklore*)

For the fourth year of the Community Engagement Residency, we instituted an application process in order to make artist selection more accessible. Quintero,

Hill, and I chose the artists. The artists that we selected, the Performance Primers (Hannah Ayasse, Chibueze Crouch, and Zoe Donnelycolt) and Jarrel Phillips, have connections to previous programs of The Bridge Project and/or my own choreographic work. Crouch is a member of the QTBIPOC Performing Artist Hive (supported by the 2018–2019 CER). Phillips performed in *Inherited Bodies*, part of *Signals from the West* (2019). Donnellycolt worked with me as a dancer in 2017. Both projects counter the isolating impacts of gentrification by bringing artists together through Capoeria (Phillips) and a curatorial platform for underserved early-career artists in Oakland (Performance Primers).

As a direct result of the last ten years of The Bridge Project's curatorial and community-building activity, HMD has profoundly changed as an organization. We have shifted—and continue to shift—to a model of distributed leadership and artist organizational power. All three co-directors are now paid the same hourly rate, which is the same rate we pay dancers who work with me. We are implementing a paid artist curatorial council. We have changed the composition of the selection panel for the Community Engagement Residency. Past lead artists now select the new CER artists, along with HMD staff of color. I have stepped off the panel. We continue to unpack where power sits within the organization. We're building relationships with funders between all three co-directors, so I as the founder don't hold those connections exclusively. We continue to discuss how to reconcile the organizational name with our commitment to decentering whiteness.

We've taken the following steps to disentangle founder personality from our broader public programs: The Bridge Project now has its own website and its own logo without "HMD" embedded in it. We are looking at re-structuring moves that will position The Bridge Project, not HMD, as the overarching organizational umbrella.

We continue to address these two questions: "How do we want artists to have power?" and "What does a radical organizational design in this area look like?" These changes are all part of our commitment to make our internal organizational structures ethical and to shift cultural power to the artists we support.

Notes

1. QTBIPOC stands for Queer Trans Black Indigenous People of Color. As of this writing, the QTBIPOC Performing Artist Hive has over eighty members. The Hive is a collective of queer and trans performing artists of color in the San Francisco Bay Area. For more information about the Hive go to https://theqtbipochive.com/ and @the.qtbipoc.hive.

2. Personal email correspondence from January 17, 2020.

3. Ariel Goldberg, *The Estrangement Principle* (Nightboat, 2016), 97–98.

4. Paul Chan, "39 Sentences," in Paul Chan, *Selected Writings 2000–2014* (Badlands Unlimited), 134.

5. Judith Butler, *Gender Trouble* (Routledge, 1999), xxii.

6. Program note for *Radical Movements: Gender and Politics in Performance*, presented by The Bridge Project, September–November 2017, on file with HMD.

7. Ursula K. LeGuin, *The Left Hand of Darkness* (Penguin, 2016), 126.

8. Rashid Johnson, as quoted in "Nine Black Artists and Cultural Leaders on Seeing and Being Seen," *NY Times Magazine*, June 27, 2020.

9. Judit Moschkovich, "—But I Know You, American Woman," in Gloria Anzaldúa and Cherie Moraga, eds., *This Bridge Called My Back: Writings by Radical Women of Color*, 2nd ed. (Kitchen Table: Women of Color Press, 1981), 79.

10. Salamishah Tillet, "Claudia Rankine Flies the Unfriendly Skies," *NY Times*, March 11, 2020, AR 18.

11. Jess Row, *White Flights: Race, Fiction, and the American Imagination* (Graywolf, 2019), 22.

12. Ibram X. Kendi, *How to be an Anti-Racist* (One World, 2019), 23.

13. Ruth Frankenberg, *White Women: Race Matters: The Social Construction of Race* (University of Minnesota Press, 1993), 156–57.

14. Over the past ten years, The Bridge Project has received support from a wide range of private foundations; city, state, and federal government sources; and individual donors. Institutional support has come from the Zellerbach Family Foundation, the Kenneth Rainin Foundation, the Walter & Elise Haas Foundation, the Phyllis C. Wattis Foundation, the Fleishhacker Foundation, the Sakana Foundation, the Center for Cultural Innovation, ODC Theater, the Doris Duke Foundation, the Erol Foundation, San Francisco Grants for the Arts,

San Francisco Arts Commission, California Arts Council, and the National Endowment for the Arts.

15. *Intersectionality* is a term created by legal scholar Kimberlé Crenshaw to refer to "the idea that multiple oppressions reinforce each other to create new categories of suffering." Keeanga-Yamahtta Taylor, *How We Get Free: Black Feminism and the Combahee River Collective* (Haymarket, 2017), 4. As a law student at Columbia, I took Constitutional Law from Crenshaw, who discussed intersectionality in depth.

16. See generally, G. William Domhoff, *Why San Francisco Is (or Used to Be) Different: Progressive Activists and Neighborhoods Had a Big Impact*, https://whorulesamerica.ucsc.edu/local/san_francisco.html; Chester Hartmann, *City for Sale: The Transformation of San Francisco*, *Revised and Updated Edition* (University of California Press, 2002); David Talbot, *Season of the Witch* (Free Press, 2013).

17. Patricia Yollin, "S.F. Could be Much Whiter in 25 Years, While the Rest of the Region Gets More Diverse," KQED News, October 26, 2015, https://www.kqed.org/news/10500291/san-francisco-could-be-a-lot-whiter-in-25-years-predicts-a-new-profile-of-bay-area (citing PolicyLink and the Program for Environmental and Regional Equity at the University of Southern California, An Equity Profile of San Francisco Bay Area Region).

18. Yollin, "S.F. Could be Much Whiter in 25 Years."

19. Yollin, "S.F. Could be Much Whiter in 25 Years."

20. Saul Alinsky, *Rules for Radicals: A Practical Primer for Realistic Radicals* (Vintage, 1971). Notably, conservative movements like the Tea Party have co-opted Alinsky's methods. See, e.g., Michael Patrick Leahy, *Rules for Conservative Radicals: Lessons from Saul Alinsky, the Tea Party Movement, and the Apostle Paul in the Age of Collaborative Technologies* (C-Rad Press, 2009).

21. Some leading texts in transformative organizing include adrienne maree brown's *Emergent Strategy: Shaping Change, Changing Worlds, Reprint ed.* (AK Press; 2017); Ejeris Dixon and Leah Lakshmi Piepzna-Samarasinha, eds., *Beyond Survival: Strategies and Stories from the Transformative Justice Movement* (AK Press, 2020); Nora Samaran, *Turn This World Inside Out: The Emergence of Nurturance Culture* (AK Press, 2019).

22. Jeff Chang, Liz Manne, and Erin Potts, "Conversation about Cultural Strategy," June 15, 2018, https://medium.com/a-more-perfect-story/a-conversation-about-cultural-strategy-9e2a28802160.

23. Nayantara Sen, *Cultural Strategy: An Introduction and Primer* (Art/Work Practice, 2019), 2; see also The Culture Group, *Making Waves: A Guide to Cultural Strategy* (2013).

24. Sen, *Cultural Strategy*, 2.

25. Sen, *Cultural Strategy*, 2.

26. See Animating Democracy/Americans for the Arts, *Aesthetic Perspectives: Attributes of Excellence in Arts for Change: Short Take* (2017), http://www.animatingdemocracy.org/sites/default/files/pictures/AestPersp/pdfs/Aesthetics%20Short%20Take.pdf.

27. See Jessica Langlois, "How Mexico's Zapatistas Inspired a Feminist, Chicana Art Movement in East L.A.," *LA Weekly*, March 3, 2017 (discussing an exhibit called "Mujeres de Maiz: Twenty

Years of ARTivism & Herstory en LA"), https://www.laweekly.com/how-mexicos-zapatistas-helped-inspire-a-feminist-chicana-art-movement-in-east-l-a/.

28. Chela Sandoval and Guisela Latorre. "Chicana/o Artivism: Judy Baca's Digital Work with Youth of Color," in Anna Everett, ed., *Learning Race and Ethnicity: Youth and Digital Media* (MIT Press, 2008), 82.

29. Guisela Latorre, "Border Consciousness and Artivist Aesthetics: Richard Lou's Performance and Multimedia Artwork," in *American Studies Journal* (2012), 57.

30. "Socially Engaged Practice," Tate Modern website, https://www.tate.org.uk/art/art-terms/s/socially-engaged-practice.

31. Randy Kennedy, "Outside the Citadel, Social Practice is Intended to Nurture," *New York Times*, March 23, 2013.

32. M. K. Asante, *It's Bigger than Hip-Hop: The Rise of the Post Hip-Hop Generation* (St. Martin's Griffin, 2009), 39.

33. Row, *White Flights*, 9.

34. Beautiful Trouble Website, https://beautifultrouble.org/tactic/legislative-theater/.

35. Row, *White Flights*, 117.

36. Laila Lalami, "Groupthink," *New York Times Magazine*, November 27, 2016, 15.

37. See Zadie Smith, "A Bird of Few Words: Narrative Mysteries in the Paintings of Lynette Yiadom-Boakye," *The New Yorker*, June 19, 2017.

38. Hilarie M. Sheets, "Black Abstraction: Not a Contradiction," *ArtNews*, June 4, 2014, 62.

39. Johnson, as quoted in "Nine Black Artists and Cultural Leaders."

40. Gerald Casel, "Gerald Casel on Responding to Trisha Brown's *Locus*," *the body is the brain* (HMD blog), November 1, 2016, https://www.hopemohr.org/blog/2016/11/1/gerald-casel-on-responding-to-trisha-browns-locus.

41. Peiling Kao, "Peiling Kao on per[mute]ing," *the body is the brain* (HMD blog), October 27, 2016, https://www.hopemohr.org/blog/2016/10/27/peiling-kao-on-permuteing.

42. See, e.g., Miguel Gutierrez, "Is Abstraction Only for White People?," *BOMB Magazine*, November 7, 2018; "On Whiteness and Abstraction: Anh Vo and Juliana May," *Critical Correspondence* (Movement Research, March 21, 2019).

43. Full statement available at *The Cut*, https://www.thecut.com/2017/08/read-kara-walkers-artists-statement-about-being-fed-up.html.

44. Jarrett Earnest, "Interview with Kelli Jones," in *What It Means to Write About Art: Interviews with Art Critics* (David Zwirner Books, 2018), 248.

45. Shannon Jackson, *Social Works: Performing Art, Supporting Publics* (Routledge, 2011), 17–18.

46. Peter Schjeldahl, "The Whitney Biennial in an Age of Anxiety," *The New Yorker*, May 20, 2019.

47. Arlene Croce, "Discussing the Undiscussable," *Writing in the Dark, Dancing in The New Yorker* (Farrar, Straus and Giroux, 2000), 708.

48. Hal Foster, "Chat Rooms" (quoting J. G. Ballard), in Claire Bishop, ed., *Participation* (Documents of Contemporary Art) (CUNY, 2004), 193

49. Wesley Morris, "Morality Wars," *NY Times Magazine* (October 3, 2018).

50. Morris, "Morality Wars."

51. manuel arturo abreu, "We Need to Talk About Social Practice," *Art Practical* (March 6, 2019).

52. Niela Orr, "Chats about Change: Ethics and Aesthetics," Artbound, February 5, 2015, https://www.kcet.org/shows/artbound/chats-about-change-ethics-and-aesthetics.

53. Orr, "Chats about Change."

54. See Sally Banes, *Terpsichore in Sneakers: Post-Modern Dance* (Wesleyan, 1987); Sally Banes, *Democracy's Body: Judson Dance Theatre, 1962–1964* (Duke University, 1993).

55. Thomas J. Lax, "allow me to begin again," in *Judson Church: The Work Is Never Done* (SFMOMA, 2018).

56. Thomas J. Lax, "allow me to begin again," in *Judson Church: The Work is Never Done* (SFMOMA, 2018) ("Judson thus contributed to making a language for ongoing experiments with dismantling male-dominated capitalist institutions, as well as for experiments supporting the black radical aesthetic tradition.").

57. Hans Obrist, as quoted in Foster, "Chat Rooms," 194.

58. Foster, "Chat Rooms," 193

59. Foster, "Chat Rooms," 194.

60. Foster, "Chat Rooms," 193.

61. Andrea Smith, "The Revolution Will Not be Funded," in INCITE, Ed., *The Revolution Will Not be Funded: The Non-Profit Industrial Complex* (Duke University Press, 2007), 9.

62. Beautiful Trouble Website, https://beautifultrouble.org/tactic/legislative-theater/.

63. Artist Campaign School, https://artistcampaignschool.org/; Artist Campaign School Promotional Video, https://vimeo.com/247441323.

64. 4Culture Website, https://www.4culture.org/grants-artist-calls/creative-consultancies/.

65. Guillermo Gómez-Peña, "Urgente! Zeitgeist SF: A Racist View on Arts Funding," *Cultural Equity Matters*, November 22, 2011, http://www.culturalequitymatters.org/?p=1.

66. manuel arturo abreu, "We Need to Talk about Social Practice," *Art Practical* (March 6, 2019).

67. Hope Mohr and Michèle Steinwald, "Building Accountability in the Dance Field: An Interview with Michèle Steinwald," *the body is the brain* (HMD blog), October 5, 2018, https://www.hopemohr.org/blog/2018/9/30/building-accountability-in-the-dance-field-an-interview-with-michele-steinwald.

68. Mohr and Steinwald, "Building Accountability."

69. Mohr and Steinwald, "Building Accountability."

70. Kendi, *How to Be an Anti-Racist*, 57.

71. A Conversation on Aesthetic Equity, Virtual Public Dialogue Presented by The Bridge Project, October 17, 2020, https://www.bridgeproject.art/public-dialogue-videos.

72. Program note for *The Unsayable*, performed March 3–6, 2011, Z Space, San Francisco, on file with HMD.

73. Adrienne Rich, "Tourism and Promised Lands," in Adrienne Rich, *Essential Essays: Culture, Politics, and the Art of Poetry* (W. W. Norton, 2018), 288.

74. Tomi Obaro, "The Great Racial Reckoning Has Begun. What Comes Next?," *BuzzFeed News*, June 11, 2020, https://www.buzzfeednews.com/article/tomiobaro/bon-appetit-crossfit-refinery29-resignations-black-lives-mat

75. Obaro, "The Great Racial Reckoning Has Begun. What Comes Next?."

76. Gerald Casel, as quoted in Sima Belmar, "In Practice: Dancing Around Race with Gerald Casel," *In Dance* (November 1, 2018).

77. Elleke Boehmer, "Transfiguring: Colonial Body into Postcolonial Narrative," *NOVEL: A Forum of Fiction* 26.3 (1993), 269.

78. David Herrera and Hope Mohr, "Race, Aesthetics, and Working in Community: From 'Dancing Around Race' to 'LatinXtensions,'" *the body is the brain* (HMD blog), October 5, 2019, https://www.hopemohr.org/blog/2019/10/4/race-aesthetics-and-working-in-community-from-dancing-around-race-to-latinxtensionsnbsp.

79. For an example of the harm that can arise between regranting organizations and the artists they support, see Nana Chinara, "An Open Letter to Arts Organizations Rampant with White Supremacy," Medium.com, May 27, 2020, https://medium.com/@nanachinara/an-open-letter-to-arts-organizations-rampant-with-white-supremacy-4540f8f0e45f.

80. See, e.g., Sarah Rafael Garcia, "Why I Resigned from the California Arts Council in the Middle of Pandemic," *Cultural Weekly*, November 2020, https://www.culturalweekly.com/why-i-resigned-from-the-california-arts-council-in-the-middle-of-a-pandemic/.

81. The "Creating New Futures" working document is available at https://creatingnewfutures.tumblr.com/. See also Dessane Lopez Cassell, "Dancers and Performers Offer 'Real Talk' on Canceled Shows, Contracts, and More," *Hyperallergic*, May 12, 2020, https://hyperallergic.com/563416/dancers-and-performers-offer-real-talk-on-canceled-shows-contracts-and-more/.

82. "Creating New Futures" working document.

83. For more information and resources about how to democratize organizational governance, see the Sustainable Economies Law Center website at https://www.theselc.org/.

84. "Continuum on Becoming an Anti-Racist Multi-Cultural Institution," Crossroads Ministry, Chicago, IL: Adapted from original concept by Bailey Jackson and Rita Hardiman, and further developed by Andrea Avazian and Ronice Branding; further adapted by Melia LaCour, https://www.aesa.us/conferences/2013_ac_presentations/Continuum_AntiRacist.pdf.

85. Race Forward Website, https://www.raceforward.org/practice/nyc-arts

86. Cyndi Suarez, *The Power Manual: How to Master Complex Power Dynamics* (New Society, 2018), 17.

87. Kendi, *How to Be an Anti-Racist*, 18.

88. Hope Mohr and Michèle Steinwald, "Building Accountability in the Dance Field: An Interview with Michèle Steinwald," *the body is the brain* (HMD blog), October 5, 2018, https://www.hopemohr.org/blog/2018/9/30/building-accountability-in-the-dance-field-an-interview-with-michele-steinwald.

89. Susan Sontag, *Regarding the Pain of Others* (New York: Picador, 2003), 101.

90. Open Mind Consulting, "Case Studies in Distributed Leadership: A Framework for Exploration, Organizational Snapshots, and Tools and Applications" (Prepared for the William and Flora Hewlett Foundation), November 2018, 13.

91. Michael Allison, Susan Misra, and Elissa Perry, "Doing More with More," *Nonprofit Quarterly*, June 25, 2018, https://nonprofitquarterly.org/doing-more-with-more-putting-shared-leadership-into-practice/ Nonprofit Quarterly.

92. Open Mind Consulting, "Case Studies in Distributed Leadership," 15.

93. Suarez, *The Power Manual*, 12.

94. Personal email exchange between Bhumi B. Patel and the author, March 10, 2020.

95. Taylor (quoting Alicia Garza), *How We Get Free*, 153.

96. Marian Taylor Brown, Hanako Brais, and Allegra Fletcher, *Toward Equity: Perspectives from Art Leaders of Color* (Arts International, September 2019), 16–17.

97. Personal email correspondence with Karla Quintero, June 16, 2020.

98. Personal email correspondence with Cherie Hill, June 15, 2020.

99. Open Mind Consulting, "Case Studies in Distributed Leadership," 4.

100. See QTBIPOC Performing Artist Hive Statement, https://www.bridgeproject.art/2019-community-engagement; see also https://theqtbipochive.com/.

101. See Leeway Foundation website, https://www.leeway.org/about/mission.

102. PSNY website, http://performancespacenewyork.org/wp-content/uploads/2020/01/02020PressReleaseWeb.pdf.

103. For discussions of more equitable and inclusive philanthropy, see Helicon Collaborative, *Not Just Money: Equity Issues in Cultural Philanthropy*, available at http://notjustmoney.us; Edgar Villanueva, *Decolonizing Wealth* (Berrett-Koehler Publishers, Inc, 2018); *Creating New Futures: Notes for Equitable Funding from Independent Arts Workers*, avail. at Creating New Futures website, https://creatingnewfutures.tumblr.com/.

104. Brown, Brais, and Fletcher, *Toward Equity*, 19.

105. Row, *White Flights*, 272.

106. Thomas DeFrantz, *Dancing Around Race*, public gathering February 28, 2019, Eric Quezada Center for Culture and Politics, San Francisco, part of Gerald Casel's 2018–2019 Community Engagement Residency, 23:15–26:28, https://vimeo.com/325326790/fcca29b129, and https://www.bridgeproject.art/2018-community-engagement.

107. Julian Carter, "Dancing Around Race: Public Gatherings #1 and #3," *Dance Matters*, April 4, 2019, https://sfdancematters.com/2019/04/14/dancing-around-race-public-gatherings-1-and-3/.

108. I take this from the wisdom, teachings, and resources of the anti-racism groups Courage of Care and Stronghold. For more information visit http://courageofcare.org/ and https://www.wearestronghold.org/.

109. See Aruna D'Souza, *Whitewalling: Art, Race, and Protest in 3 Acts* (Badlands, 2018) (setting forth case studies in how white allyship has failed in the visual arts world).

110. Row, *White Flights*, 275.

111. Row, *White Flights*, 275.

112. See Julietta Singh, *Unthinking Mastery: Dehumanism and Decolonial Entanglements* (Duke University Press, 2018), 9. Thanks to Julie Tolentino for bringing this book to my attention.

113. INCITE, *The Revolution Will Not Be Funded*, 15.

114. Thomas DeFrantz, *Dancing Around Race*, 30:13–30:37.

115. Steve Paxton, "Improvisation Is a Word for Something That Can't Keep a Name," *Contact Quarterly* (1987, Spring/Summer), 15–19.

116. Paxton, "Improvisation Is a Word"; Malaika Sarco-Thomas, "touch + talk: Ecologies of Questioning in Contact and Improvisation," *Journal of Dance & Somatic Practices* 6: 2 (2014), 193–197.

117. QTBIPOC Performing Artist Hive mission statement, The Bridge Project website, https://www.bridgeproject.art/2019-community-engagement. See also https://theqtbipochive.com/.

118. Suarez, *The Power Manual*, 11.

119. Garrett Hongo, *The Mirror Diary: Selected Essays* (University of Michigan Press, 2017), 155.

120. Adrienne Rich, "Conditions for Work: The Common World of Women," in *On Lies, Secrets, and Silence: Selected Prose 1966–1978* (W. W. Norton, 1979), 204.

121. Jenny Odell, *How to Do Nothing: Resisting the Attention Economy* (Melville House, 2019), 159.

122. Rich, "Conditions for Work," 214.

123. Michelle LaVigne and Megan V. Nicely, "Curating Dialogue: The Bridge Project's Radical Movements," *TDR/The Drama Review*, 62:4 (NYU and MIT Press, Winter 2018), 150.

124. Maura Reilly, *Curatorial Activism: Towards an Ethics of Curating* (Thames & Hudson, 2018), 31.

125. Sara Ahmed, *Living a Feminist Life* (Duke University Press, 2017), 18.

126. See Cherie Hill, "Aesthetic Equity Workshop with Liz Lerman and Paloma McGregor: Photo Essay and Participant Response," *the body is the brain* (HMD blog), November 17, 2019, https://www.hopemohr.org/blog/2019/11/17/participant-response-aesthetic-equity-workshop-with-liz-lerman-amp-paloma-mcgregor-oct-26-2019.

127. Anonymous workshop participant feedback in response to post-workshop survey, on file with HMD.

128. Anonymous workshop participant feedback in response to post-workshop survey, on file with HMD.

129. Personal email exchange between Bhumi B. Patel and the author, March 10, 2020.

130. Transcript of community question circle, part of *Reorganizing Ourselves*, at the Joe Goode Annex, San Francisco, November 7, 2015, co-presented by The Bridge Project and CounterPulse, 0:40–2:52, https://www.bridgeproject.art/public-dialogue-videos and through YouTube at https://youtu.be/yaWIHWr8P9s.

131. LaVigne and Nicely, "Curating Dialogue," 147.

132. LaVigne and Nicely, "Curating Dialogue," 146.

133. LaVigne and Nicely, "Curating Dialogue," 146–147.

134. LaVigne and Nicely, "Curating Dialogue," 147.

135. Sima Belmar, "In Practice: Body Nerds: Judith Butler and Monique Jenkinson," *In Dance*, January 1, 2018.

136. Transcript of performance of *Ordinary Practices of the Radical Body*, created and performed by Judith Butler and Monique Jenkinson, November 3, 2017, at CounterPulse, San Francisco, as part of *Radical Movements: Gender and Politics in Performance*, commissioned by HMD's The Bridge Project. Private video on file with HMD. Video timecode 2:13–20:56.

137. Maxe Crandall and Selby Schwartz, "Radical Movements: Gender and Politics in Performance," *Critical Correspondence*, December 14, 2017, https://movementresearch.org/publications/critical-correspondence/radical-movements-gender-and-politics-in-performance.

138. See Paper Monument, *As radical, a mother, as salad, as shelter: What should art institutions do now?* (Paper Monument, 2018).

139. Hope Mohr and Julie Tolentino, "Reflections on Julie Tolentino's Community Engagement Residency," *the body is the brain* (HMD blog), April 1, 2018, https://www.hopemohr.org/blog/2018/3/27/julies-tolentinos-2017-community-engagement-residency.

140. Mohr and Tolentino, "Reflections."

141. Crandall and Schwartz, "Radical Movements: Gender and Politics in Performance."

142. Lavigne and Nicely, "Curating Dialogue," 152.

143. The Lab and HMD's Bridge Project co-presented *.bury.me.fiercely.* at The Lab on February 18, 2018, in partnership with SFMOMA's Open Space / Limited Edition, featuring Julie Tolentino and fellow performers Stosh Fila aka Pigpen, Cirilo Domine, and Marc Manning, live sound.

144. Mohr and Tolentino, "Reflections."

145. Mohr and Tolentino, "Reflections."

146. Here I discuss about refusal in the arts, but refusal in other disciplines is instructive. See, e.g., Tuck, Eve, and K. Wayne Yang. "R-Words: Refusing Research," in *Humanizing Research: Decolonizing Qualitative Inquiry with Youth and Communities*, edited by Django Paris and Maisha Winney (Sage, 2013), 223–48; Audra Simpson, "The Ruse of Consent and the Anatomy of 'Refusal': Cases from Indigenous North America and Australia," in *Postcolonial Studies* 20, no. 1 (January 2, 2017), 18–33.

147. Nicolas Bourriaud, *Relational Aesthetics* (Les Presse Du Reel, 1998). Bourriaud defined "relational aesthetics" as a "set of artistic practices which take as their theoretical and practical point of departure the whole of human relations and their social context, rather than an independent and private space." Tate Modern website, http://www.tate.org.uk/learn/online-resources/glossary/r/relational-aesthetics.

148. Caroline Hamilton, Michelle Kelly, Elaine Minor, eds. *The Politics and Aesthetics of Refusal* (Cambridge Scholars, 2007), 6.

149. Jackson (quoting Bishop), 47; Claire Bishop, "Antagonism and Relational Aesthetics," *October* (Fall 2004), 110.

150. See, e.g., Joanne Barker, "The Specters of Recognition," in *Formations of United States Colonialism*, ed. Alyosha Goldstein (Duke University Press, 2014); Brian Klopotek, *Recognition Odysseys: Indignity, Race, and Federal Recognition in Three Louisiana Indian Communities* (Duke University Press, 2011); Glen Coulthard, *Red Skin, White Masks: Rejecting the Colonial Politics of Recognition* (University of Minnesota Press, 2014).

151. Jack Halberstam, *The Queer Art of Failure* (Duke University Press, 2011), 88.

152. See, e.g., Robert Morris, "Unavailable," (2011), https://orienteering.tumblr.com/post/20761189903/unavailable-robert-morris-2011.

153. Lucy Lippard, "Trojan Horses: Activist Art and Power," in Brian Wallis, ed., *Art after Modernism: Rethinking Representation* (David R. Godine, Reprint ed., 1984), https://voidnetwork.gr/wp-content/uploads/2016/09/Trojan-Horses-Activist-Art-and-Power-Lucy-Lippard.pdf.

154. Randy Kennedy, "Outside the Citadel, Social Practice is Intended to Nurture," *New York Times*, March 23, 2013, https://www.nytimes.com/2013/03/24/arts/design/outside-the-citadel-social-practice-art-is-intended-to-nurture.html?_r=0.

155. Deena Chalabi, "A Method for Public Reimagining: Move Slowly and Knit Things Together," *Public Knowledge*, SFMOMA, June 25, 2019, https://publicknowledge.sfmoma.org/a-method-for-public-reimagining-move-slowly-and-knit-things-together/.

156. I use the term "white supremacy" in this book to refer to the dominant form of racism in the United States. bell hooks persuasively argues that "white supremacy" is a better term for the exploitation of people of color than "racism" because it explicitly names the link between racism and white privilege. See Trina Grillo and Stephanie M. Wildman (quoting bell hooks), "Obscuring the Importance of Race: The Implication of Making Comparisons between Racism and Sexism (or Other Isms)," in *Critical Race Feminism: A Reader* (NYU Press, 1997), 45.

157. Kenneth Jones and Tema Okun, "White Supremacy Culture," in *Dismantling Racism: A Workbook for Social Change Groups* (ChangeWork, 2001); https://www.showingupforracialjustice.org/white-supremacy-culture-characteristics.html.

158. Personal email exchange between Bhumi B. Patel and the author, March 9, 2020.

159. Transcript of performance of *dance of darkness: a performance, a conversation, a rehearsal for the future*, created and performed by boychild and Jack Halberstam, November 4, 2017, at CounterPulse, San Francisco, as part of *Radical Movements: Gender and Politics in Performance*, commissioned by HMD's The Bridge Project, 1:16:00–1:19:00, https://vimeo.com/247062899.

160. Sen, *Cultural Strategy*, 21.

161. Sen, *Cultural Strategy*, 21.

162. Sen, *Cultural Strategy*, 21.

163. Transcript of performance of *dance of darkness: a performance, a conversation, a rehearsal for the future*, created and performed by boychild and Jack Halberstam, November 4, 2017, at CounterPulse, San Francisco, as part of *Radical Movements: Gender and Politics in Performance*, commissioned by HMD's The Bridge Project, 1:08:04–1:09:53, https://vimeo.com/247062899.

164. For further reading about Julie Tolentino's work, see Gigi Otálvaro-Hormillosa, "Entangled Vulnerabilities: Julie Tolentino's *.bury.me.fiercely.*," SFMOMA's Open Space, March 20, 2018, https://openspace.sfmoma.org/2018/03/entangled-vulnerabilities-julie-tolentinos-bury-me-fiercely/; Hentyle Yapp, "To Punk, Yield, and Flail: Julie Tolentino's Etiolations and the Strong Performative Impulse," *GLQ* (2018) 24 (1): 113–138.

165. See The Bridge Project's Community Engagement Residency website, https://www.bridgeproject.art/community-engagement-residency.

166. Reni Eddo-Lodge, *Why I'm No Longer Talking to White People About Race* (Bloomsbury, 2017), 155.

167. Personal conversation between David Herrera and author, November 12, 2020.

168. Jenny Odell, *How to Do Nothing: Resisting the Attention Economy* (Melville House, 2019), 173.

169. Odell, *How to Do Nothing*, 162.

170. Claire Bishop, *Artificial Hells: Participatory Art and the Politics of Spectatorship* (Verso, 2012), 255.

171. Sen, *Cultural Strategy*, 24.

172. Robin DiAngelo, *White Fragility: Why It's So Hard for White People to Talk About Racism* (Beacon Press, 2018); Kenneth Jones and Tema Okun, *Dismantling Racism: A Workbook for Social Change Groups* (ChangeWork, 2001); see also People's Institute for Survival and Beyond, "Attributes of White Organizational Culture," https://heller.brandeis.edu/segal/pdfs/white-supremacy-culture.pdf.

173. See Sara Ahmed, "Queer Feelings," *Routledge Queer Studies Reader*, Donald Hall et al., eds. (Routledge, 2013). ("Discomfort is crucial if we want to challenge norms and envision possibilities for collective living."); Liz Lerman, *Hiking the Horizontal* (Wesleyan, 2011), 6.

174. Sen, *Cultural Strategy*, 22.

175. Kendi, *How to be an Anti-Racist*, 237.

176. The Bridge Project website, "Community Engagement Residency," https://www.bridgeproject.art/2019-community-engagement.

177. Personal email exchange between Karla Quintero and author, March 2019.

178. Sima Belmar, "In Practice: Dancing Around Race with Gerald Casel," *In Dance*, November 1, 2018.

179. See Lois Weaver website, http://www.split-britches.com/longtable ("The Long Table is a dinner party structured by etiquette, where conversation is the only course. The project

ingeniously combines theatricality and models for public engagement. It is at once a stylised appropriation and an open-ended, nonhierarchical format for participation. Both of these elements—theatrical craft and political commitment—are mutually supporting in this widely and internationally toured work. The (often-feminised) domestic realm here becomes a stage for public thought.").

180. Bhumi B. Patel, *Reflection: Dancing Around Race Public Gathering, Life of a Modern Dancer* (blog), March 2019.

181. Personal email exchange between Karla Quintero and author, March 2019.

182. Personal email exchange between Bhumi B. Patel and the author, March 9, 2020.

183. Julian Carter, "Dancing Around Race: Public Gatherings #1 and #3," *Dance Matters* (April 4, 2019), https://sfdancematters.com/2019/04/14/dancing-around-race-public-gatherings-1-and-3/; see also Yayoi Kambara, "Dancing (In)Equity," *the body is the brain* (HMD blog), September 12, 2018, https://www.hopemohr.org/blog/2018/9/12/inequity.

184. Internal feedback offered by Gerald Casel to HMD, on file with HMD.

185. George Lipsitz, "The Racialization of Space and the Spatialization of Race," *Landscape Journal* 26(1): 10–23; see also George Lipsitz, *The Possessive Investment in Whiteness: How White People Profit off Identity Politics* (Temple University Press, 2006).

186. DiAngelo, *White Fragility*.

187. Personal email exchange between Bhumi B. Patel and the author, March 10, 2020.

188. LaVigne and Nicely, "Curating Dialogue," 148.

189. LaVigne and Nicely, "Curating Dialogue," 149.

190. Judith Butler, *Gender Trouble: Feminism and the Subversion of Identity* (Routledge, 2011); Molly Fischer, "Think Gender Is Performance? You Have Judith Butler to Thank for That," *New York Magazine*, June 13, 2016.

191. Butler, *Gender Trouble*, 19–20.

192. Katherine Profeta, *Dramaturgy in Motion: At Work on Dance and Movement Performance* (University of Wisconsin Press, 2015), 171.

193. Triple Canopy website, https://www.canopycanopycanopy.com/contents/on-value; Ralph Lemon, *On Value* (Triple Canopy, 2016).

194. Claire Bishop, "The Year in Performance," *Art Forum*, December 2014, https://www.artforum.com/print/201410/claire-bishop-49123

195. Triple Canopy website, https://www.canopycanopycanopy.com/contents/on-value; Ralph Lemon, *On Value* (Triple Canopy, 2016).

196. Meg Stuart, *Damaged Goods* website, http://www.damagedgoods.be/auf-den-tisch.

197. Robert Avila, "A philosopher and a drag queen meet on a dance floor...", *48 Hills* (December 7, 2017).

198. Performance Practice.org, http://performancepractice.org/portfolio/paramodernities/.

199. David E. Moreno, "Paramodernities," *Culture Vulture* (February 23, 2018).

200. Sebert, "In 'Paramodernities.'"

201. Personal email correspondence between Netta Yerushalmy and the author, April 1, 2020.

202. Transcript of performance of *dance of darkness: a performance, a conversation, a rehearsal for the future*, created and performed by boychild and Jack Halberstam, November 4, 2017, at CounterPulse, San Francisco, as part of *Radical Movements: Gender and Politics in Performance*, commissioned by HMD's The Bridge Project, 10:43–11:05, https://vimeo.com/247062899.

203. Transcript of performance of *dance of darkness*, 8:35–8:45.

204. LaVigne and Nicely, "Curating Dialogue," 149.

205. See Gilles Deleuze and Félix Guattari, *A Thousand Plateaus: Capitalism and Schizophrenia* (University of Minnesota Press, 1987), 378.

206. See, e.g., James C. Scott, *Weapons of the Weak: Everyday Forms of Peasant Resistance* (Yale University Press, 1987).

207. Transcript of performance of *dance of darkness: a performance, a conversation, a rehearsal for the future*, created and performed by boychild and Jack Halberstam, November 4, 2017, at CounterPulse, San Francisco, as part of *Radical Movements: Gender and Politics in Performance*, commissioned by HMD's The Bridge Project, 45:00-1:01:20, https://vimeo.com/247062899.

208. Profeta, *Dramaturgy in Motion*, 173.

209. Transcript of Simone Forti performing her News Animations as part of *Have We Come a Long Way, Baby?*, September 27, 2016, Joe Goode Annex, San Francisco, presented by The Bridge Project. https://vimeo.com/108380308/54112a10ba. Video timecode 13:00–13:45.

210. Row, *White Flights*, 190.

211. Maria Lind, ed., *Performing the Curatorial: Within and Beyond Art* (Sternberg Press, 2012), 13.

212. Johan Oberg, "Performing Heritage at the University," in *Performing the Curatorial: Within and Beyond Art* (Sternberg Press, 2012), 8.

213. Suzanna Friscia, "Are We Too Precious with Classic Dance Works?" *Dance Magazine* (January 2020).

214. Harold Bloom, *The Anxiety of Influence: A Theory of Poetry* (Oxford University Press, 2d. ed., 1997).

215. Claudia Rankine, "Teju Cole's Essays Build Connections between African and Western Art," *New York Times Book Review*, August 12, 2016.

216. Netta Yerushalmy, from "Rethinking Dance Landmarks: An Interview with Netta Yerushalmy about Paramodernities," https://medium.com/odc-dance-stories/rethinking-dance-landmarks-an-interview-with-netta-yerushalmy-about-paramodernities-8cd146fb603c, February 21, 2018.

217. Hope Mohr, Larry Arrington, Gerald Casel, Gregory Dawson, Peiling Kao, Xandra Ibarra, and Margo Moritz, "Choreographic Transmission in an Expanded Field: Reflections on 'Ten Artists Respond to Trisha Brown's *Locus*,'" *TDR/The Drama Review*, 62:2 (NYU and MIT Press, Summer 2018), 143–150.

218. Reilly, *Curatorial Activism*, 15.

219. Reilly, *Curatorial Activism*, 33.

220. Brian Sebert, "In 'Paramodernities,' Words and Dance Do Battle. The Audience Wins," *New York Times*, March 15, 2019.

221. Heather Desaulniers, "The Bridge Project 2014," September 28, 2014, http://www.heatherdance.com/2014/09/the-bridge-project-2014.html.

222. Transcript of post-show discussion after *Have We Come a Long Way, Baby?* on September 27, 2014, Joe Goode Annex, San Francisco, featuring Anna Halprin, Simone Forti, and Hope Mohr, moderated by Professor Janice Ross. Presented by The Bridge Project, 23:00–25:00, https://vimeo.com/108208157.

223. Transcript of post-show discussion after *Have We Come a Long Way, Baby?*, 2:00–4:36.

224. Personal email exchange between Peiling Kao and author, March 15, 2020.

225. See, e.g., Gerald Casel, "Gerald Casel on Responding to Trisha Brown's Locus," *the body is the brain* (HMD blog), November 1, 2016, https://www.hopemohr.org/blog/2016/11/1/gerald-casel-on-responding-to-trisha-browns-locus; Peiling Kao, "Peiling Kao on per[mute] ing," *the body is the brain* (HMD blog), October 27, 2016, https://www.hopemohr.org/blog/2016/10/27/peiling-kao-on-permuteing.

226. Christina Sharpe, *In the Wake* (Duke University Press, 2016), 100.

227. Mohr et al., "Choreographic Transmission in an Expanded Field," 250.

228. Comment by the artist during residency at ODC Theater for *Signals from the West: Bay Area Artists in Conversation with Merce Cunningham*, August 2020.

229. Notes from first artist gathering as part of *Signals from the West: Bay Area Artists in Conversation with Merce Cunningham*, on file with HMD.

230. Notes from second artist gathering as part of *Signals from the West: Bay Area Artists in Conversation with Merce Cunningham*, on file with HMD.

231. Leena Joshi, "The Sounds We're Hearing Are Those of a Gay Ghost," *Open Space*, SFMOMA, December 9, 2019, https://openspace.sfmoma.org/2019/12/the-sounds-were-hearing-are-the-sounds-of-a-gay-ghost/.

232. Personal email exchange between Rashaun Mitchell and the author, June 20, 2018.

233. Sam Lefebvre, "Merce Cunningham Artist Residency Celebrates, Challenges Dance Luminary," *KQED Arts,* August 26, 2019. For other reviews of the program, see Melissa Hudson Bell, "Dancing with a Ghost: Bay Area artists honor Merce Cunningham, " *SF Chronicle,* November 4, 2019; Leena Joshi, "The Sounds We're Hearing Are the Sounds of a Gay Ghost" *Open Space*, SFMOMA, December 09, 2019; Garth Grimball, "A Bridge to Cunningham in Six Quotations, " *Life as a Modern Dancer*, November 26, 2019; Sima Belmar, "An Invitation to Stumble, " *ODC Dance Stories*, November 16, 2019.

234. LeFebvre, "Merce Cunningham Artist Residency."

235. Comment by the artist during artist residency at ODC Theater for *Signals from the West: Bay Area Artists in Conversation with Merce Cunningham*, August 2020.

236. Comment by the artist during artist residency at ODC Theater for *Signals from the West*.

237. Comment by the artist during artist residency at ODC Theater for *Signals from the West*.

238. Comment by the artist during artist residency at ODC Theater for *Signals from the West*.

239. Joan Acocella, "Can Modern Dance Be Preserved?," *The New Yorker*, July 1, 2019.

240. Comment by the artist made during artist residency at ODC Theater for *Signals from the West*.

241. Comment by the artist made during artist residency at ODC Theater for *Signals from the West*.

242. Silas Riener, Rashaun Mitchell, and Claudia LaRocco, "Already & Not Yet: Rashaun Mitchell and Silas Riener in Conversation with Claudia La Rocco," *Open Space*, SFMOMA (November 7, 2019), https://openspace.sfmoma.org/2019/11/already-not-yet-rashaun-mitchell-and-silas-riener-in-conversation-with-claudia-la-rocco/

243. Riener, Mitchell, and LaRocco, "Already & Not Yet."

244. Riener, Mitchell, and LaRocco, "Already & Not Yet."

245. Riener, Mitchell, and LaRocco, "Already & Not Yet."

246. Riener, Mitchell, and LaRocco, "Already & Not Yet."

247. Aruna D'Souza, speaking as part of the On Whiteness Symposium, Racial Imaginary Institute, June 30, 2018, https://theracialimaginary.org/on-whiteness-symposium-june-30th/.

248. Profeta, *Dramaturgy in Motion*, 173.

249. Joshi, "The Sounds We're Hearing Are Those of a Gay Ghost," 200.

250. Sontag, *Regarding the Pain of Others*, 68.

251. Animating Democracy/Americans for the Arts, Aesthetic Perspectives: Attributes of Excellence in Arts for Change: Short Take (2017) (quoting Rise Wilson), http://www.animatingdemocracy.org/sites/default/files/pictures/AestPersp/pdfs/Aesthetics%20Short%20Take.pdf.

252. MAP Fund, *Diving into Racial Equity: The MAP Fund's Exploration*, 13, https://mapfundblog.org/animating-democracy-collaboration/, https://mapfundblog.org/wp-content/uploads/2019/12/Diving-into-Racial-Equity_MAP-AD.pdf.

253. Kendi (quoting Ashley Montagu), *How to Be an Anti-Racist*, 91.

254. Gerald Casel, "Gerald Casel on Responding to Trisha Brown's Locus," *the body is the brain* (HMD blog), November 1, 2016, https://www.hopemohr.org/blog/2016/11/1/gerald-casel-on-responding-to-trisha-browns-locus.

255. Ibid.

256. Racial Imaginary Institute website, https://thekitchen.org/event/on-whiteness-exhibition.

257. Charmian Wells, "Strong and Wrong: On Ignorance and Modes of White Spectatorship in Dance Criticism," in *Critical Correspondence*, Movement Research, June 30, 2017, https://movementresearch.org/publications/critical-correspondence/strong-and-wrong-on-ignorance-and-modes-of-white-spectatorship-in-dance-criticism.

258. Thomas DeFrantz, Dancing Around Race public gathering, February 28, 2019, Eric Quezada Center for Culture and Politics, San Francisco, part of Gerald Casel's 2018–2019

Community Engagement Residency. Video avail. at https://vimeo.com/325326790/fcca29b129 and https://www.hopemohr.org/2018-community-engagement. Video timecodes 15:35 and 17:25–19:30.

259. MAP Fund, https://mapfundblog.org/wp-content/uploads/2020/02/2020-by-the-Numbers.pdf.

260. Syeda Malliha and Lauren Slone, *2020 by the Numbers*, Map Fund Website, https://mapfundblog.org/wp-content/uploads/2020/02/2020-by-the-Numbers.pdf.

261. Sustainable Arts Foundation website, https://www.sustainableartsfoundation.org/racial-equity; Caroline and Tony Grant, "I Once Was Blind: Acknowledging Race in Granting to Individuals," Grantmakers in the Arts website, https://www.giarts.org/i-once-was-blind.

262. Grant, "I Once Was Blind."

263. Tschabalala Self, as quoted in "Nine Black Artists and Cultural Leaders on Seeing and Being Seen," *NY Times Magazine*, June 27, 2020.

264. Virginia Woolf, *A Room of One's Own* (Harvest/HBJ, 1929), 56–57.

265. Liberation psychology is based on the premise that a person's experience is intrinsically connected with sociopolitical structures. The field of liberation psychology originates in the work of Brazilian educator Paulo Freire, who coined the term *concientización*, which translates roughly as the raising of political consciousness. See Paulo Freire, *Pedagogy of the Oppressed* (Continuum, 30th Anniversary ed., 2000); see also Ignacio Martín-Baró, *Writings for a Liberation Psychology*, Adrianne Aron and Shawn Corne, eds. (Harvard University Press, 1994).

266. Row, *White Flights*, 241.

267. Rich, "Tourism and Promised Lands," 288.

268. Hilton Als, "The Soullessness of 'Straight White Men,'" *The New Yorker*, August 6 & 13, 2018 (emphasis mine).

269. Adrienne Rich, "What Does a Woman Need to Know?" in Adrienne Rich, *Essential Essays: Culture, Politics, and the Art of Poetry* (W. W. Norton, 2018), 151.

270. Adrienne Rich, "Blood, Bread, and Poetry," in Adrienne Rich, *Essential Essays: Culture, Politics, and the Art of Poetry* (W. W. Norton, 2018), 245.

271. Ahmed, *Living a Feminist Life*, 13.

272. Mick Maslen and Jack Southern (quoting Cornelia Parker), *The Drawing Projects: An Exploration of the Language of Drawing* (Black Dog Publishing, 2011).

273. Rich, "Tourism and Promised Lands," 288.

274. Paul Chan, "The Rewriting of the Disaster," in *Selected Writings 2000–2014* (Badlands Unlimited), 32.

275. See, e.g., Miguel Gutierrez, "Is Abstraction Only for White People?"; "On Whiteness and Abstraction: Anh Vo and Juliana May," *Critical Correspondence*, Movement Research, March 21, 2019.

276. Michèle Steinwald, "Building Accountability in the Dance Field," *the body is the brain* (HMD blog), October 5, 2018.

277. Steinwald, "Building Accountability."

278. I use the term decolonization mindful that the term refers literally to the return of stolen lands to indigenous and colonized peoples and that work in the cultural sector is not a substitute for economic and political reparations. See Eve Tuck and K. Wayne Yang, "Decolonization is not a Metaphor," in *Decolonization: Indigeneity, Education & Society* Vol. 1, No. 1, (2012), 1–40.

279. Row, *White Flights*, 81.

280. Row, *White Flights*, 23.

281. Row, *White Flights*, 33.

282. Row, *White Flights*, 65.

283. Row, *White Flights*, 70–71.

284. Row, *White Flights*, 78.

285. Diane Arbus, quoted in *Diane Arbus: Revelations* (Random House, 203), 54.

286. Jarrett Earnest, "Interview with Chris Kraus," in *What it Means to Write About Art: Interviews with Art Critics* (David Zwirner Books, 2018), 261.

287. Adrienne Rich, "Six Meditations in Place of a Lecture," in Adrienne Rich, *Essential Essays: Culture, Politics, and the Art of Poetry* (W. W. Norton, 2018), 293.

288. Zadie Smith, "Lynette Yiadom-Boakye's Imaginary Portraits," *The New Yorker*, June 19, 2017.

289. Smith, "Lynette Yiadom-Boakye's Imaginary Portraits" (emphasis mine).

290. Taney Roniger, "In Praise of Form: Towards a New Post-Humanist Art," *Interalia Magazine*, September 2019, https://www.interaliamag.org/articles/taney-roniger/.

291. Adrienne Rich, "Blood, Bread, and Poetry," 240.

292. Reis Thebault, Andrew Ba Tran, and Vanessa Williams, "The Coronavirus Is Infecting and Killing Black Americans at an Alarmingly High Rate," *The Washington Post*, April 7, 2020.

293. Adrienne Rich, "Poetry and The Forgotten Future," in Adrienne Rich, *Essential Essays: Culture, Politics, and the Art of Poetry* (W. W. Norton, 2018), 240.

294. This set of exercises is adapted from the wisdom, teachings, and resources of the anti-racism goups Courage of Care and Stronghold. For more information visit http://courageofcare.org/ and https://www.wearestronghold.org/.

295. I recognize that the process of decolonization refers literally to the return of stolen lands to indigenous peoples. In using the term "decolonize," I do not intend to obscure the importance of the real and necessary process of returning stolen lands to native people.

296. I am grateful to my collaborators and colleagues Karla Quintero, Belinda He, Jane Selna, Natalya Shoaf, Suzette Sagisi, Yayoi Kambara, David Herrera, Julie Tolentino, and Gerald Casel, among many others doing the work of decolonizing dance. See, e.g., Emmaly Wiederholt, "Questioning Neutrality and Colonization in Contemporary Dance: An Interview with Gerald Casel," *Stance on Dance*, December 8, 2016; http://stanceondance.com/2016/12/08/questioning-neutrality-and-colonization-in-contemporary-dance/; Suzette Sagisi, "Embodied Feeling, Intentionality, and Decolonizing Movement," *the body is the brain,* September 23, 2020

(discussing her process with choreographer Maurya Kerr making the dance BLACKSTAR), https://www.hopemohr.org/blog/2020/9/22/on-decolonizing-movement-embodied-feeling-and-intentionality.

297. For a playful discussion of the intertwined lineages of Anna Halprin, Judson Dance Theater, and Merce Cunningham, see Silas Riener, Rashaun Mitchell, and Claudia LaRocco, "Already & Not Yet: Rashaun Mitchell and Silas Riener in Conversation with Claudia La Rocco," *Open Space*, SFMOMA (November 7, 2019), https://openspace.sfmoma.org/2019/11/already-not-yet-rashaun-mitchell-and-silas-riener-in-conversation-with-claudia-la-rocco/.

298. Audience Readers from The Bridge Project, including Readers from *Radical Movements: Gender and Politics in Performance* (2017); *Dancing Around Race* (2018); and *Signals from the West: Bay Area Artists in Conversation with Merce Cunningham at 100* (2019), are available at https://www.bridgeproject.art/community-readers.

299. Aruna D'Souza, *Whitewalling: Art, Race, and Protest in 3 Acts* (Badlands, 2018).

300. Americans for the Arts has defined cultural equity as, "embodying the values, policies, and practices that ensure that all people—including but not limited to those who have been historically underrepresented based on race/ethnicity, age, disability, sexual orientation, gender, gender identity, socioeconomic status, geography, citizenship status, or religion…—are represented in the development of arts policy; the support of artists; the nurturing of accessible, thriving venues for expression; and the fair distribution of programmatic, financial, and informational resources." Americans for the Arts, Statement on Cultural Equity (October 26, 2016), https://www.americansforthearts.org/about-americans-for-the-arts/cultural-equity.

Acknowledgments

Thank you to Christy Bolingbroke at the National Center for Choreography for making this book possible, to Michèle Steinwald for editorial support, and to Thea Ledendecker at The University of Akron Press for shepherding the process. Deep gratitude to Cherie Hill, Safi Jiroh, and Karla Quintero for their partnership, vision, and generosity in our shared work of distributed leadership. Thank you to the following creative changemakers who have been valued colleagues in the ongoing work of organizational and social transformation: Hannah Ayasse, Gerald Casel, Julian Carter, Tristan Ching, Maxe Crandall, Chibueze Crouch, Zoe Donnellycolt, Daria Garina, David Herrera, Tracy Taylor Grubbs, Belinda He, Catherine Honig, Yayoi Kambara, Jen Norris, Ranu Mukherjee, Parker Murphy, Bhumi B. Patel, Jane Selna, Suzette Sagisi, Leslie Ziegler Schrock, David Szlasa, Jarell Phillips, Estrellx Supernova (formerly known as randy reyes), Julie Tolentino, and Megan Wright. Thank you to Anna, Jackson, and Matt for giving me sanctuary.

Index of Artists Cited